Backyards for Kids

A *Sunset* Outdoor Design & Build Guide

By Lisa Taggart and the Editors of *Sunset*

Sunset

©2012 by Time Home Entertainment Inc.
135 West 50th Street, New York, NY 10020

ISBN-13: 978-0-376-01436-8   ISBN-10: 0-376-01436-9
Library of Congress Control Number: 2011936510
First printing 2011. Printed in the United States of America.

OXMOOR HOUSE
VP, PUBLISHING DIRECTOR: Jim Childs
EDITORIAL DIRECTOR: Susan Payne Dobbs
CREATIVE DIRECTOR: Felicity Keane
BRAND MANAGER: Fonda Hitchcock
MANAGING EDITOR: Laurie S. Herr

SUNSET PUBLISHING
PRESIDENT: Barb Newton
VP, EDITOR-IN-CHIEF: Katie Tamony
CREATIVE DIRECTOR: Mia Daminato
ART DIRECTOR: James McCann

**Outdoor Design & Build Guide: _Backyards for Kids_
CONTRIBUTORS**
MANAGING EDITOR: Bridget Biscotti Bradley
PHOTO EDITOR: Philippine Scali
DESIGN AND PRODUCTION: Suzanne Scott
PRODUCTION SPECIALIST: Linda M. Bouchard
PRODUCTION ASSISTANT: Danielle Johnson
ILLUSTRATOR: Damien Scogin
PROOFREADER: John Edmonds
PROJECT EDITOR: Sarah H. Doss
INDEXER: Marjorie Joy
TECHNICAL ADVISER: Scott Gibson
IMAGING SPECIALIST: Kimberley Navabpour
SERIES DESIGN: Susan Scandrett

To order additional publications, call 1-800-765-6400
For more books to enrich your life, visit **oxmoorhouse.com**
Visit Sunset online at **sunset.com**
For the most comprehensive selection of Sunset books, visit **sunsetbooks.com**
For more exciting home and garden ideas, visit **myhomeideas.com**

IMPORTANT SAFETY WARNING—PLEASE READ

contents

Inspiration

page 4

Browse this chapter for ideas on realizing your own perfect space to create moments you will cherish.

How to Build

page 70

Review step-by-step instructions for 15 projects to create your own family fun. We have a range of projects, both simple and challenging.

Finishing the Look

page 136

In these pages, you'll find tips on planning, basic construction and materials, decorating playhouse interiors, sports fields, family gardens, and more.

Inspiration

We all need playtime in our lives. You want your backyard to be about you—your space, your family, your fun. Make room for games, fantasy, and good times with a miniature dream house, a soccer field, or a rope swing. The magic of the yards pictured here is in the imaginations they capture: a hobbit house in the forest, a secret fort safe from intruders, a gentle swing under an elm with a river view. Where do you want to spend your afternoons? Unleash your creativity and dream up the most fun you can have in your own backyard. Get inspired on these pages and build a perfect playland with help from *Sunset*'s expert builders and designers. If you build it, they will play. Let the fun begin!

Find joy in your own backyard by creating space for play.

make room for play

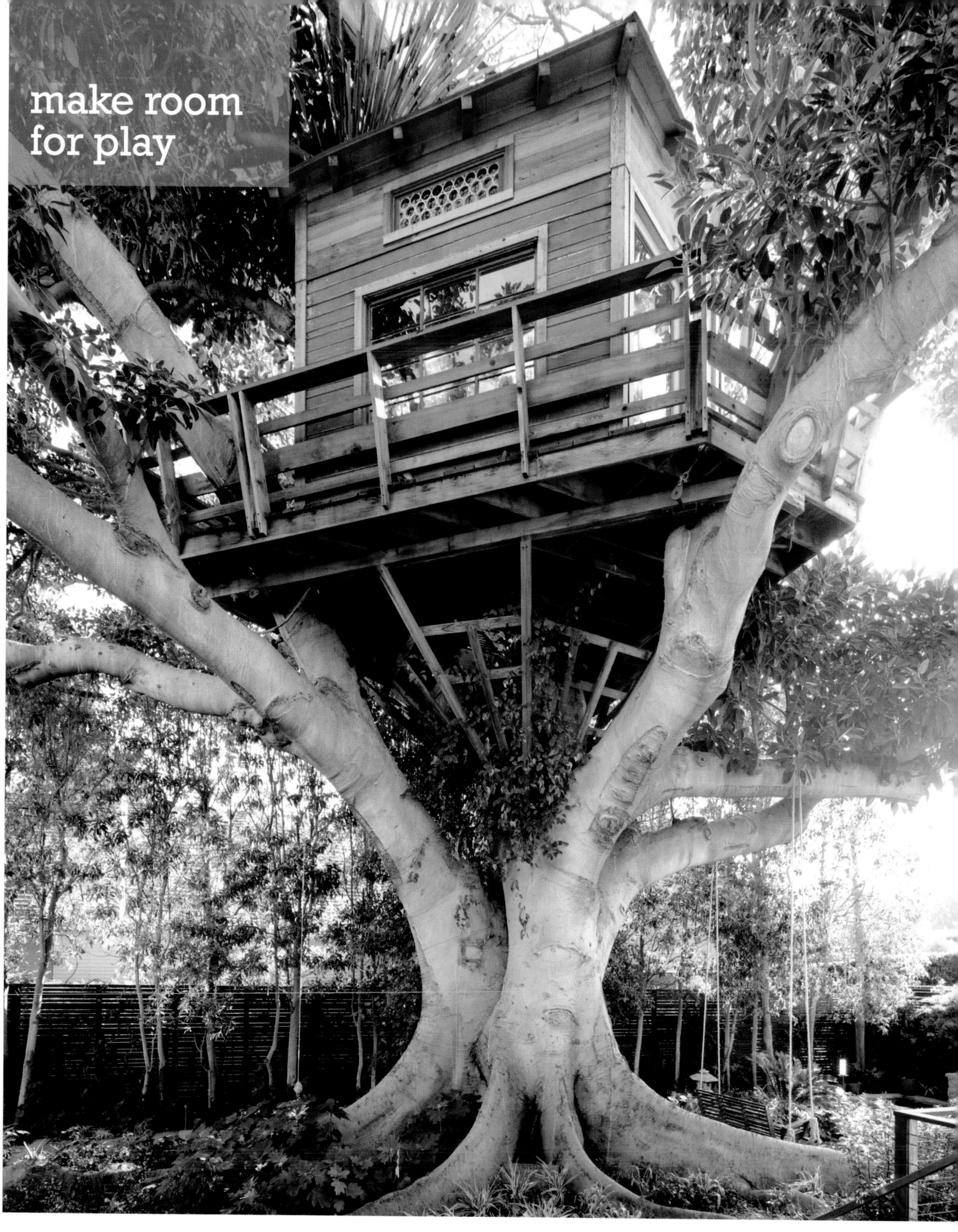

LEFT: Talk about a playful tree! This house offers a great lookout view and a balcony too. Large windows let in plenty of light. Below, a swing hangs in a dreamy spot. The structure, designed to work in harmony with the tree's geometry, is well supported by branches and boards.

ABOVE: A hammock is more fun when it's shared with a friend.

RIGHT: Build a space where your child can be creative.

inspirational spaces

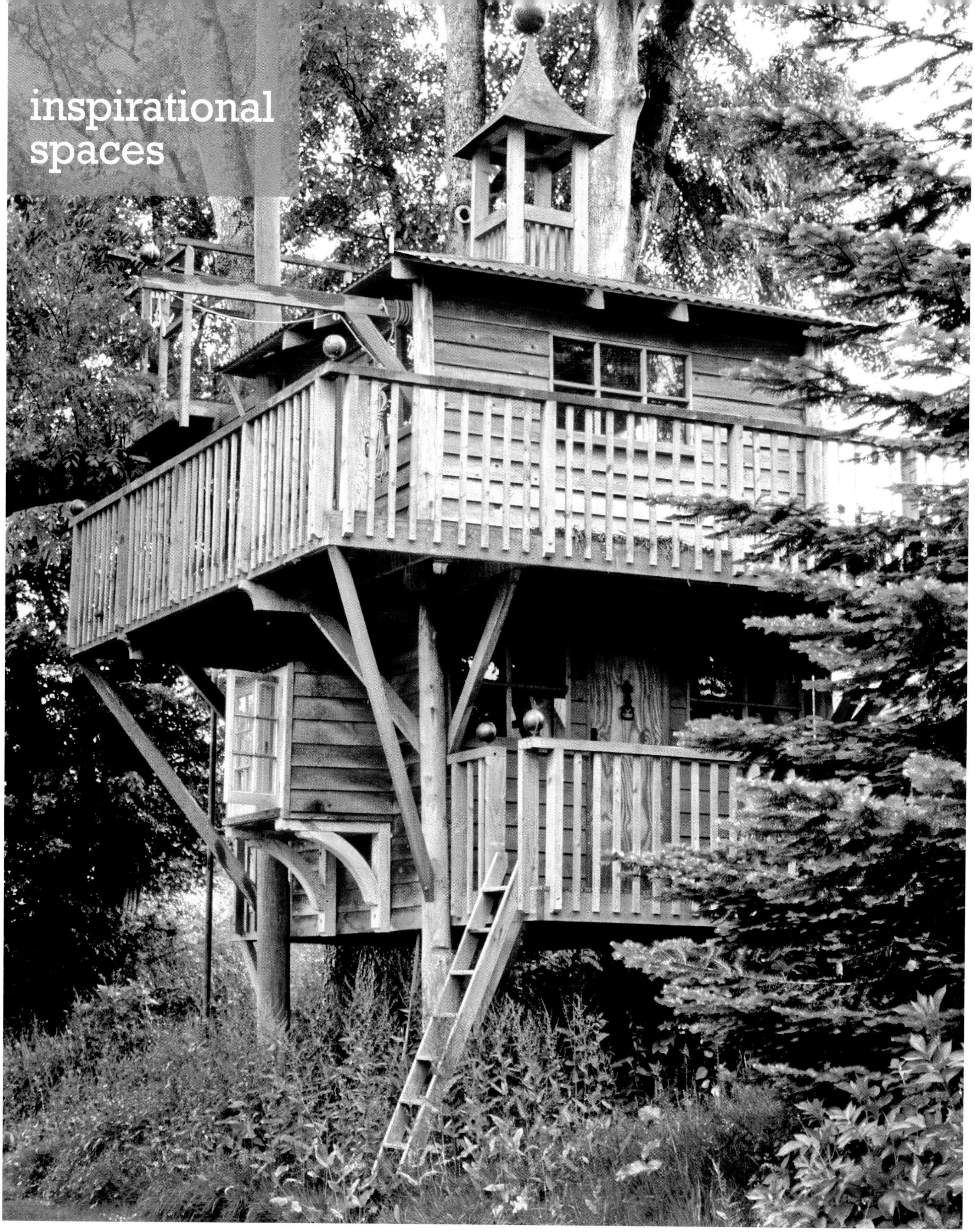

LEFT: This ultimate elevated playhouse has two stories, a ladder entry, wrap-around decks, and a watch-tower for playing pirate one day and backwoods explorer the next. Natural wood looks right in this forest setting.

TOP RIGHT: Small house, outsized charm. Climbing jasmine and a white picket fence are a romantic pairing for this cottage. Add a garden setting, Dutch door, and casement windows for Old World ambiance.

BOTTOM RIGHT: Inside is just as sweet. Matching twin beds under the eaves are a nice spot for a sleepover.

cottage charmers

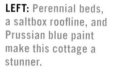

LEFT: Perennial beds, a saltbox roofline, and Prussian blue paint make this cottage a stunner.

BOTTOM LEFT: A tiny cottage covered by climbing roses is a sweet place for a tea party. Natural log framing and not-quite-square corners add to the sense of whimsy.

BOTTOM RIGHT: A loft corner softened by pillows makes a cozy reading nook.

Miniature Adirondack rockers are just right for this porch. The windows, window box, and table and chairs inside are scaled to size as well.

11

home sweet small home

The perfect playhouse has all the features of a grown-up house, scaled small. Window boxes and checked curtains add fairy tale charm to this tiny chocolate and lime green structure.

ABOVE: An A-frame with attitude. Everything is brightly colored here: The hot pink porch and lanterns and yellow planter boxes make it a standout in the garden.

LEFT: A living sod roof, dotted with flowers, adds to the fantastical nature of the house.

LEFT: Slightly hidden by perennials and stone slabs, a modern airy retreat promises refuge at path's end.

RIGHT: Woven reeds partially screen this garden fort.

design lesson

>> Depending on what size playhouse you plan to add to your yard, you may need to obtain a building permit. Be sure to contact your local planning department before you start building.

make an entrance

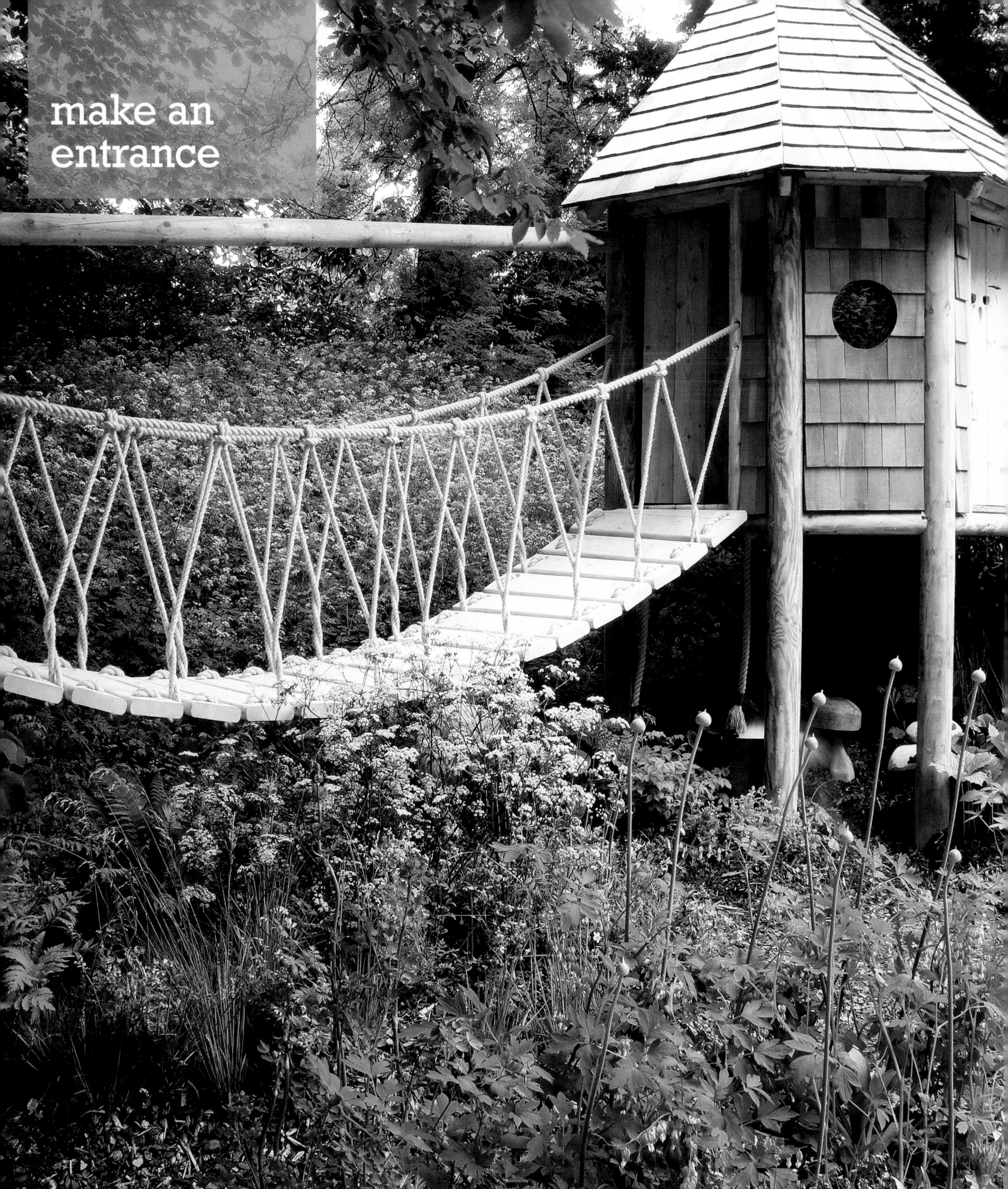

LEFT: A clatter bridge with rope rails and a porthole window means no surprise intruders to this six-sided play-house.

RIGHT: An ogee arch doorway with diamond peephole and an octagonal side window provide an exotic look to this retreat.

BELOW: Stone steps and a transition to gravel mulch separate the playhouse from the vegetable garden. Tree stumps just outside the playhouse offer end-less opportunities for jumping, hiding, and climbing.

in the round

Alice in Wonderland might find one of her friends under this bell-shaped thatch roof. A concrete dragon guards the entry.

TOP LEFT: What tiny creature lives in this tree trunk?

TOP RIGHT: A circular metal frame holds wood slat siding for this round two-story hideaway. The platform above is the perfect place for secret clubhouse meetings.

BELOW: A simple fabric tent gains punch with polka dots.

a leafy
view

LEFT: After a snooze in the hammock or a snack at the table, climb the ladder to this rustic cabin with end-cut wood siding, Tudor windows, and reed roof. The wavy ballusters add charm, but should be spaced no more than 4³/₈ inches apart to meet safety standards.

RIGHT: Skyward nautical: A clatter bridge leads to a forest outpost with porthole windows. The sinuous rope handrail on the deck echoes the nautical touches with ocean-like ripples.

BELOW: A simple elevated structure can change themes as kids grow.

This fantastic Queen Anne structure in the redwoods features a six-sided turret, board-and-batten siding, multipaned windows, ornate pediments, matchstick railings, and Doric columns, creating an elevated masterpiece of play.

LEFT: Climbing roses, wisteria, and potted herbs make a verdant entryway to this hip-roofed cottage at tree height. Six-paned French doors add elegance and let in light.

BOTTOM LEFT: A tree-house with room for sleepovers is ideal. Exposed framing doubles as shelving.

BOTTOM RIGHT: Way up the trunk of this tree is a simple platform with an A-frame roof. Only the nimble-footed climber can visit.

ABOVE: Rest your head on a daybed surrounded by a dozen pillows.

LEFT: A rustic cabin with an air mattress provides a place for quiet naps in the trees.

RIGHT: A sweet little play area is just right perched on a hillside with an expansive vineyard view.

Tudor windows shroud the goings-on of royal playmakers. Note the window pattern is echoed in the trellis and zigzag brickwork.

Careful where you wander in fantasy landscapes. Knights and pirates can be in the most unexpected places.

tunnels
and ropes

ABOVE: Crawl in! This landscape makes playtime the first priority.

OPPOSITE, TOP: A winding path ends in a serpent's tail, where children can take a shortcut back to the start through a tunnel. Succulent plantings prevent erosion and add pops of color while echoing the circular designs.

OPPOSITE, BOTTOM LEFT: Walls worthy of Spider-Man are supported by pipe and metal O hooks. Shredded bark is a soft surface for landings.

OPPOSITE, BOTTOM RIGHT: A wood-and-rope tunnel practically begs you to climb in.

swing
into it

LEFT: Common seat materials for swings include flexible plastic, tires, canvas, and wood.

ABOVE: A giant basket swing is roomy enough for two. The soft material and natural shape provide a pleasing contrast to the lines of the house and deck.

design lesson

Swing seats made of rubber or plastic are lighter than ones made of metal or wood. The heavier the seat, the more painful the collision with a child. Try bucket or belt seats of rubber, canvas, plastic, or polyethylene.

ABOVE: Be sure to leave at least 24 inches between adjacent swing seats.

LEFT: A summer afternoon on a swing is a pure distillation of childhood joy.

OPPOSITE: A wood slat bench with metal frame makes a good swing for sharing.

play structures

SUNSET CONTRIBUTING EDITOR
PETER O. WHITELEY ON

soft landings

» Be sure there's adequate cushioning at the base of your play structures. Layers of sand, pea gravel, mulch, or wood chips are recommended. Needed depth varies by material.

LEFT: A rustic play structure with an elevated platform, slide, and swing blends into this apple orchard.

ABOVE: Shade-tolerant plants soften the lines between garden and play space.

RIGHT: A tiered herb garden leads to this log-framed structure tucked into a corner of the hillside yard. Mulch reduces weeds and provides a soft surface underfoot.

slide
along

LEFT: Water + slide = fun summer days.

RIGHT: A poured concrete slide is a tempting shortcut to the sunken yard for kids and adults alike. A rope anchored to the grassy slope offers an alternative way down.

BELOW: This metal slide is screened by bamboo. Consider sun exposure when choosing your slide material.

sandboxes

sizing sandboxes

» An ideal sandbox is about 4 feet by 8 feet, but smaller ones can work too. They should be filled with at least a foot of sand to allow for real digging. Choose sterilized play sand and cover when not in use to protect from animals.

ABOVE: A circular sandbox in a garden setting is edged by a pond. Adding water to sand, of course, maximizes the fun.

TOP RIGHT: Railroad ties enclose this sandbox and provide bench seating.

BOTTOM RIGHT: Even babies enjoy supervised time in the sandbox.

You want a lawn that's
nice to flop down on!

LEFT: Raised beds and steppingstones in crushed granite separate activity areas in this yard. The raised beds at the far end help protect plants from stray balls.

BELOW: Grass that can be cut short makes the best surface for soccer.

SUNSET GARDEN EDITOR
KATHLEEN NORRIS BRENZEL ON

grass

» For speed, grass on a soccer field should be mowed short: 0.75 to 1.5 inches. Bermuda grass is the most popular choice, but choose the grass that will thrive best in your climate and exposure.

jump

LEFT: Trampolines unleash exuberance like nothing else. They require adequate space and a soft landing surface.

ABOVE: Jump rope doesn't need much space at all. While it's easy to do solo, it's more fun with the whole family. Here, the alternating squares of grass and hardscape mark the entry and set a playful tone.

design lesson

» Trampolines require careful planning and adult supervision. Pads over the springs or full enclosures are two options for making them safer. Consider in-ground trampolines for young children (see page 159).

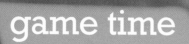

LEFT: The serious game of chess lightens up with oversized pieces on the lawn.

RIGHT: Chalkboard paint can turn an ordinary wall into an artist's drawing board, or a large canvas for a family game of hangman.

BELOW: Bowling works in a small space. Wood decking informally marks the lanes.

relaxation
station

LEFT: The sound and sight of splashing water appeal to all ages.

ABOVE: With room for two plus a stuffed lion and warm blankets, this hammock has everything a good nap requires.

RIGHT: In their own private space, children can explore their creativity.

SUNSET HEAD GARDENER
RICK LAFRENTZ ON

water sounds

» Surround yourself with soothing sound: The murmur of falling water is calming and can lull you to sleep on a summer afternoon. Install a fountain or other water feature near your favorite napping hammock or relaxation space.

LEFT: An outdoor dining nook has benches and plenty of cushions. Extras are nearby.

RIGHT: Clumping grass is a cushiony surface—and doesn't need mowing.

BELOW: Here the whole family can relax outdoors, with durable woven resin furniture, cushions, and a cozy outdoor bean bag. Slate tiles form a surface for a hopscotch game.

design lesson

❯❯ Soft surfaces like grass and cushions invite relaxation. Choose weather-resistant fabrics for upholstery, or take cushions indoors when they are not in use.

hop in

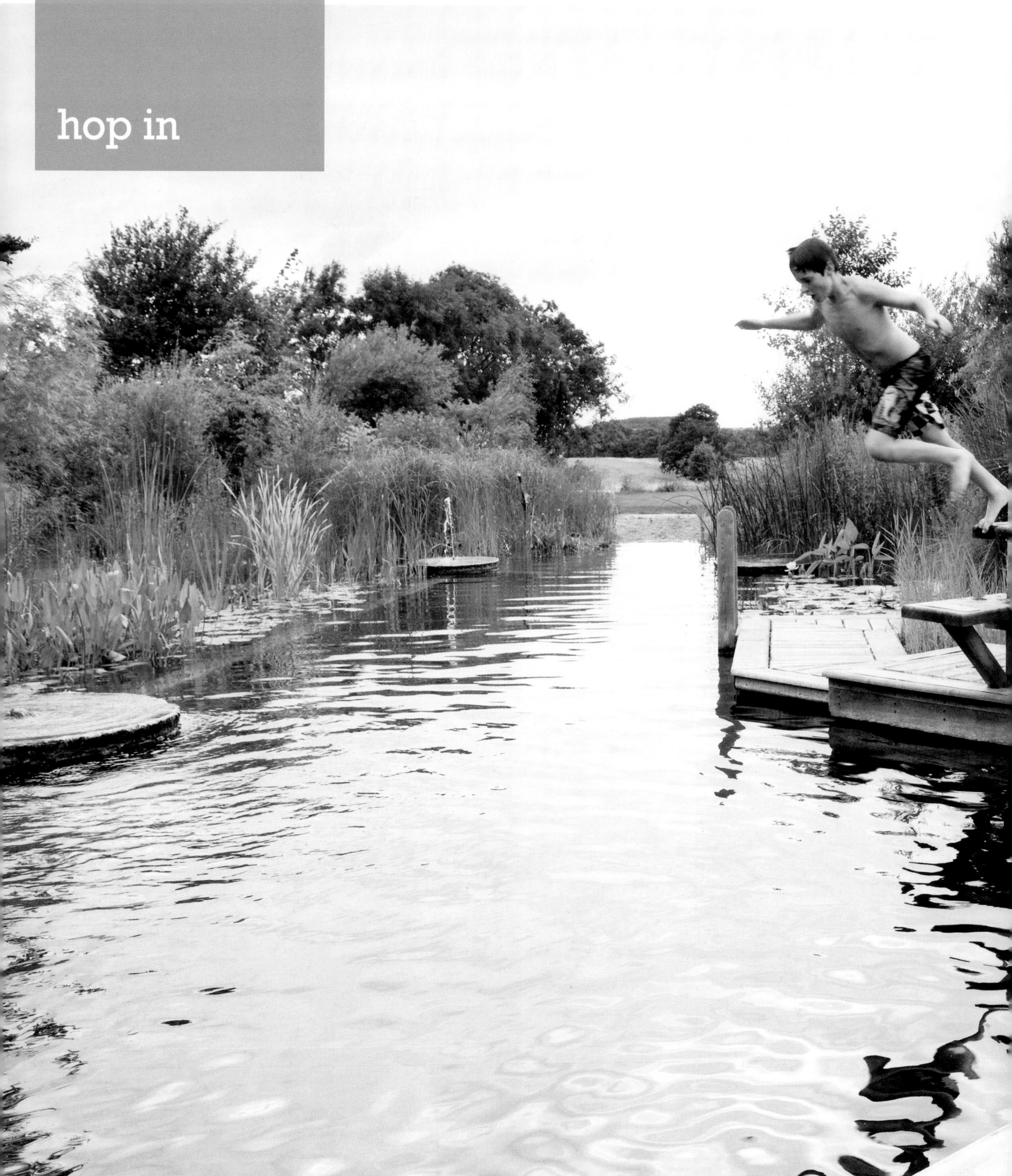

LEFT: If you are fortunate enough to have a natural water feature on your property, enjoy it!

ABOVE: Support wildlife such as frogs, toads, and birds by avoiding chemical fertilizers and pesticides.

RIGHT: Summer's riches: popsicles and a swimming pool.

LEFT: No one stays dry for long at this swimming pool.

ABOVE: Here's an above-ground pool that doesn't compromise on elegance. A glass wall allows you to see swimmers in action.

LEFT: At the beach, a quick rinse removes sand and seawater.

RIGHT: Tropical foliage forms a privacy screen in this backyard oasis.

BELOW: Outdoor showers are a summer delight. They can also help keep houses clean by reducing the amount of dirt tracked in.

LEFT: Tucked between a playhouse and a hedge, a simple shower with a wooden platform offers a fresh-air rinse.

ABOVE: Why not an outdoor tub? A swirling mosaic tile pattern and claw feet add to the al fresco fun.

RIGHT: Building an outdoor shower can be as simple as connecting a showerhead to a garden hose. Or the shower can be plumbed to provide warm water. To avoid rot, seal wooden platforms so that water beads up on the surface instead of penetrating the wood.

LEFT: Growing your own produce makes family meals tastier while increasing appreciation and respect for vegetables.

RIGHT: Gardens are natural learning labs for kids.

ABOVE: Different shapes and textures entrance kids of all ages. Brightly colored veggies and blooms are eye-catching.

LEFT: Be sure to let your little ones get their hands dirty!

RIGHT: Playful shapes support these vegetables and engage children's imaginations.

SUNSET GARDEN
EDITOR KATHLEEN
NORRIS BRENZEL ON

edibles

》 Get your kids involved early in planning your garden. Plant their favorite vegetables and have them help water and weed. Tough, fast-growing plants are the easiest to appreciate. Try sunflowers, squash, beans, and cucumbers.

LEFT: Teamwork gets the apricot picking done.

ABOVE: As children get older, they can help with more garden tasks. Sorting and cleaning vegetables is a good activity to help them appreciate dinner.

RIGHT: Nurturing plants from seed teaches patience and builds a sense of accomplishment.

LEFT: Even the family dog wants in on the circle of play. The circle will change but keep the playful energy constant.

ABOVE: Children can take a role in caring for chickens. Have them help at feeding time and collect eggs.

RIGHT: Take time to delight in the visitors that come to your yard.

set a playful tone

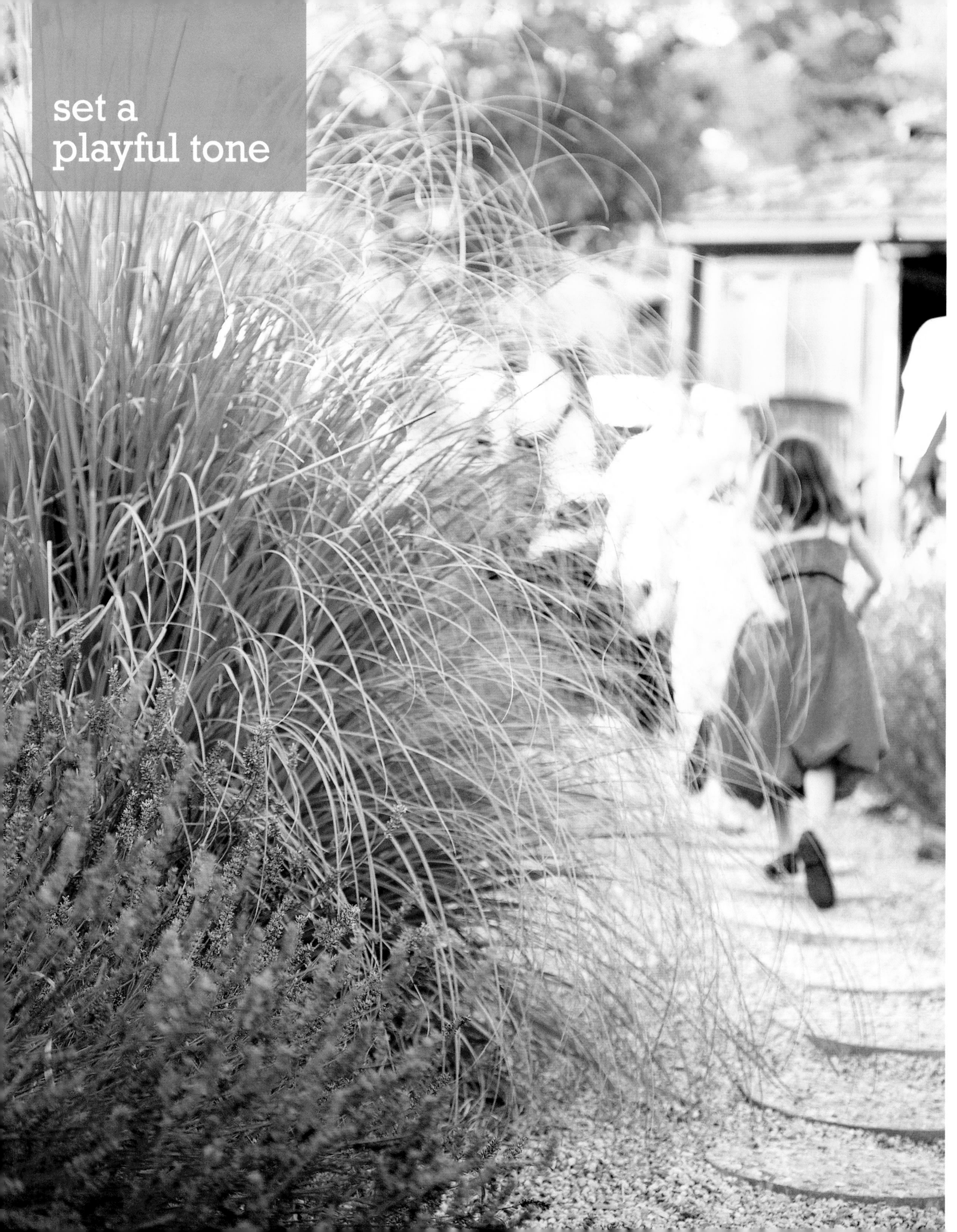

LEFT: What appeals to young garden visitors is a sense of possibility and discovery. High grasses and a path that curves off ahead spark curiosity.

ABOVE: You want your backyard to be a place for celebrating all sorts of milestones.

RIGHT: Why construct an ordinary screen when you can be more creative? Painted pointed columns resemble oversized pencils.

LEFT: Your backyard needs will change over time. Adapt by making small adjustments to your plantings, surfacing, and furniture.

ABOVE: After all, fun is where you find it—and make it.

How to Build

Are you ready to create the playful backyard of your dreams? We've assembled 15 projects ranging from simple ones that you can build yourself to more complex ones that require professional assistance. Of course you can customize the designs and materials for your yard and your family's needs. We also have tips on designing for kids, building safely, and using tools alongside your family. In just a few weekends you can have a new playhouse, fort, or sandbox that will capture your child's imagination for years.

Build it and they will come! Welcome play into your yard with a structure made by you.

designing
for kids

The porch of this playhouse is a nice spot for cupcakes and tea.

The backyard is a place for your child to while away a summer afternoon, to dabble and doodle, to conjure up enchanted creatures and fantastical story lines, to be free of the schedule-focused concerns of school and practices, and to build moments that will be a future adult's most cherished memories. The most essential ingredient for this is giving your child space to dream.

Constructing a landscape that ignites the imagination is a tall order. For some plans, you will need to jump into the details of materials, architectural designs, construction, and building codes—but it's also possible to create engaging spaces that allow for open-ended play and require little or no structure at all.

Getting Them Involved

Be sure to work with your child in creating your designs. Getting your child involved can increase the fun and will certainly add to everyone's satisfaction with the final result. Sketch or build plans together. Use a Lego kit or building blocks, or try constructing models out of popsicle sticks, toothpicks, cardboard, or balsa wood.

Choosing the Site

Before you settle on any particular location, step back and consider the whole yard. Make a drawing or site map, marking dimensions. Note details such as areas with strong sun or wind, the location of pipes and utility lines, and any trees or plants that cannot be moved.

As you begin construction, consider views and sight lines from all sides of the lot. You may want to:

» Make sure you can supervise the play area from a deck or an inside room.
» Remove obstructions such as a pole or an overgrown tree that could block your view.
» Consider foot traffic through play, garden, and sitting areas.
» Screen undesirable views to the street or a neighbor's home.
» Build a fence or plant hedges as a safety, privacy, or sound barrier.

Take on a small project together.

JOBS FOR KIDS Getting them involved safely

Letting children participate in building their own play spaces sounds like a great idea, but it can end in frustration or injury if you don't think it through.

That's not to say avoid family projects entirely. Just pace yourself and gauge your patience level. Follow our guidelines for age-appropriate tasks to keep your expectations realistic. Keep safety in mind at all times. Even when kids are watching you use a power tool, or if you are doing something that produces chips or flying bits, make sure the kids also have safety goggles on.

3–5 years
» Help design
» Hold tape measure
» Hand over nails or tools
» Fetch items
» Shovel sand or gravel
» Paint
» Help clean up

6–7 years
All of the above, plus:
» Drill, with adult supervision
» Tighten screws in predrilled holes
» Tighten bolts
» Sort parts
» Note and check measurements
» Help check for square angles
» Remove nails, with adult supervision

8–11 years
All of the above, plus:
» Nail
» Mix concrete (one sack at a time)
» Cut boards to lengths with a hand saw, where angle isn't critical and with adult supervision

12 years and older
» Most construction tasks, depending on the child
» Power saw with jigsaw if wood is clamped and adult is watching
» More complex saw cuts, with adult supervision
» Independent drilling

What Kid-Size Means at Different Ages

Age	Doorway height	Guardrail height	Rung spacing*
2–3½ years	32–43 inches	22–24 inches	9–18 inches
5½–6½ years	38–51 inches	22–29 inches	14–27 inches
11½–12½ years	52–69 inches	30–39 inches	18–31 inches

Age	Chin bar height**	Minimum seat width	
2–3½ years	38–49 inches	6–9 inches	
5½–6½ years	46–62 inches	7–11 inches	
11½–12½ years	62–84 inches	9–16 inches	

*On horizontal ladders, monkey bars
**Where feet bottom out

LEFT: Let your child hold the nail. Hand-eye coordination keeps him from hitting his fingers with the hammer.

RIGHT: Involve your child in the building process and you'll both feel greater satisfaction at project's end.

sod-roof cabin

Designer and builder:
Bob Stanton

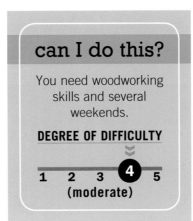

This simple play cabin has board-and-batten walls, a sod roof, recycled leaded glass windows, and a Dutch door. It was designed for a 7-year-old girl, with a plan that in later years it could be converted into a garden shed. The flowering roof reminded the owners of cottages they saw on a trip to Norway.

Design

To maximize ceiling space in the minimal structure, the builder used three beams instead of the usual roof trusses for support. This gives the cabin enough head room for adults so that it can be converted to a shed later. Over the beams he nailed car decking, 2 x 6 boards with tongue-and-groove edges. Their interlocking design adds strength and stability.

can I do this?

You need woodworking skills and several weekends.

DEGREE OF DIFFICULTY

1   2   3   **4**   5
(moderate)

WHAT YOU'LL NEED

Concrete pier blocks to support floor

Pressure-treated beams

Pressure-treated joists

Joist hangers

Sheets of 1½"-thick exterior plywood

Decking material

Framing for walls

Boards and battens for siding

Corner and trim boards

Door and jamb

Windows

Galvanized nails

See page 82 for materials needed for the sod roof.

BUILDING THE CABIN

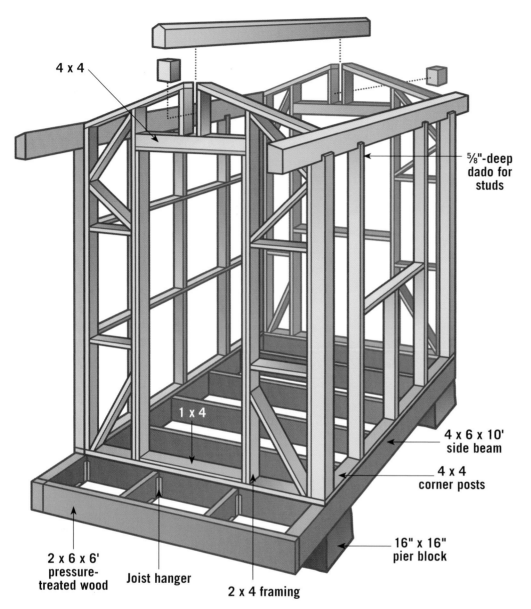

4 x 4

⅝"-deep dado for studs

1 x 4

4 x 6 x 10' side beam

4 x 4 corner posts

16" x 16" pier block

2 x 6 x 6' pressure-treated wood

Joist hanger

2 x 4 framing

❶ Build the Floor

Clear the site. Install four concrete pier blocks recessed into the ground so that their top surfaces are level. Attach 2 x 6 floor joists to side beams with joist hangers. Joists are doubled under end walls of the cabin. Fit the plywood floor flush with the outside perimeter of the framing and fasten with nails.

❷ Cut Dadoes

Three substantial roof beams allow for a truss-free roof. Cut ⅝-inch-deep dadoes for the side-wall studs. The easiest method is to first make multiple passes with a circular saw, leaving approximately ⅛ inch between cuts. Use a chisel to clean out the cut.

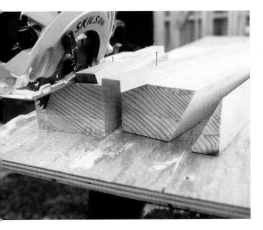

❸ Bevel the Side Beams

A circular saw may not cut deeply enough on first pass to accommodate the slope of this roof. To bevel the side beams adequately, tack a guide piece onto the beam and make the cut, as shown. Then flip the beam over and cut through the rest of the way to wind up with the piece shown on the right.

❹ Build the Walls

Frame the walls on the floor to get the right fit. The side walls run the full length of the floor, while the end walls equal the width minus the space needed for the side walls. Because the playhouse has board-and-batten siding, the framing includes 2-by-4-inch blocking at two heights.

❺ Raise the Walls

After building the framing for both side walls, nail the board-and-batten siding to the far wall's exterior. Leave a nail's width between each board. The batten nails fit into the gaps between the boards, whose edges are held down by the battens. Once the boards and battens are attached, tilt the wall into place. With diagonal bracing holding the wall steady, nail through the bottom plate to secure the wall to the floor. Then raise, brace, and nail the other side wall. See page 145 for more information on board-and-batten siding.

❻ Reinforce the Roof

There is no framing for the roof except along the end walls, where 2 x 4 braces keep the roof weight from pushing the side walls apart.

❼ Cut the Decking

Trim the car decking boards to length and to the roof angle.

❽ Build the Roof

After trimming off the groove edge on the end pieces, nail the car decking into place. For most of the pieces, nails go only into the beams. But over the end walls, also nail the car decking to the top brace piece in the wall framing.

BUILDING THE SOD ROOF

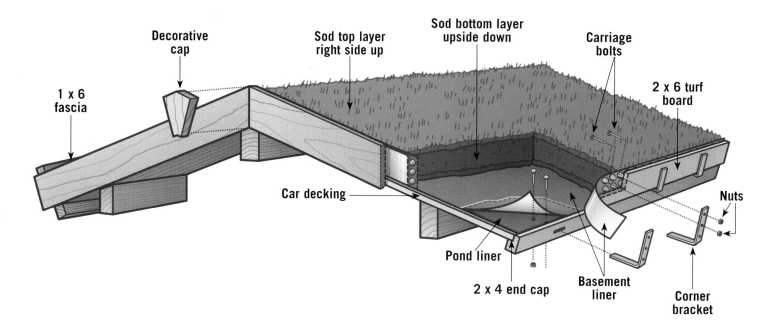

Decorative cap

Sod top layer right side up

Sod bottom layer upside down

Carriage bolts

1 x 6 fascia

2 x 6 turf board

Car decking

Nuts

Pond liner

2 x 4 end cap

Basement liner

Corner bracket

Design

The key elements to a sod roof are waterproofing and ensuring adequate support. A plastic pond liner covering the roof serves as a waterproof membrane. Over that, a dimpled plastic sheet (normally used for waterproofing basements) adds protection. Parallel grooves formed in the plastic point downhill, channeling rainwater off the roof. Two layers of turf are rolled out over that, the first with the grass side down, the second with the grass side up. The plastic sheet's dimples create airspace on the back and give the grass roots something to grip on the front.

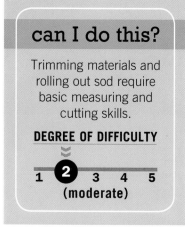

can I do this?

Trimming materials and rolling out sod require basic measuring and cutting skills.

DEGREE OF DIFFICULTY

1 **2** 3 4 5
(moderate)

WHAT YOU'LL NEED

Beams

Car decking pieces cut to length

Pressure-treated turf boards

Pressure-treated fascias

End caps

Pond liner sheet

Basement water-channel liner

Sod

Duct tape

Galvanized corner brackets

Galvanized carriage bolts with nuts

Galvanized nails

❶ Create a Slot to Set the Gap

Drill small side-by-side holes to create a slot for the corner brackets, then slip the brackets through (see illustration). Use a small piece of each of the plastic materials as a spacer for aligning the brackets. Set the gap between the turf board and the roof wide enough to allow both plastic layers to fit underneath.

❷ Tack the Waterproofing

With the turf board in place, drape the pond liner over the roof and pull up the front and back edges to cover the 1 x 6 fascia pieces on the eaves. To keep the membrane from flopping down, tack it in place along the upper edge of the rake edges only. The main roof expanse has no fasteners, so nothing compromises the waterproofing.

❸ Install the Second Layer

The basement waterproofing layer comes in a roll. Cut two pieces, one for each side of the roof, and then smooth them in place, positioning them so the dimples run downhill. At the ridge, tape the pieces together with duct tape. At the bottom, push the plastic down so that it extends past the edge of the roof deck and touches the metal brackets. The membrane curls up along the rake edges, protecting the wood.

❹ Lay the Sod

Unroll the sod just like carpet. The first layer goes grass side down, the top layer grass side up. Arrange the layers so that joints do not overlap. For the first layer, begin with a piece cut in half crosswise. For the second, start with a piece cut in half lengthwise. Tuck in roots along the edges to avoid a patchwork look.

❺ Plant in Gaps

After a week or two, fill in any gaps with handfuls of soil. Scatter seeds of grass and low-growing wildflowers, or add more mature plants.

SUNSET SENIOR GARDEN EDITOR JULIE CHAI ON

green roofs

❱❱ A sod roof filters pollution, acts as insulation for heat and noise, reduces runoff, and provides an ecosystem for insects and birds. You can add low-growing native wildflowers for extra color and to support wildlife. Choose plants that will thrive in your climate. If the summers are dry in your area, poke bits of sedum or other succulents into the sod. They will root and spread, allowing the roof to remain green even during drought. Sod roofs don't need to be mowed, but they may need to be raked every few years to remove excess thatch.

elevated
cabin

An elevated shed-roof playhouse with rustic charm, this structure has plenty of fun notes, including shutters on the lower level, a peek hole, a mailbox, and lucky charms affixed to the siding.

Design

Built with wood from old fences and decks, windows from a salvage yard, and a door from a circa-1900 Victorian house, this playhouse has woodsy cabin appeal and is eco-conscious. There's room for play below and above. With magnolia branches edging the back of the cabin, the children have lots of privacy and access to climbing. And clear corrugated plastic roofing lets in daylight.

can I do this?

Constructing an elevated playhouse with deck and stairway requires advanced woodworking skills. This structure is a two- or three-person job and will take several weekends.

DEGREE OF DIFFICULTY

1   2   3   **4**   5
(moderate)

4 x 4 support posts, preferably redwood

2 x 4s, 2 x 6s, 4 x 4s for framing, preferably redwood

1 x 8 for siding; can be reclaimed wood

2 x 6 decking boards

2 x 8 joists for deck

4 x 4 railing posts

Rails; can be reclaimed

Braces for deck

Clear corrugated plastic sheeting for roof

2 x 10s for stairs

Joist hangers

Deck screws

Concrete mix

Lag bolts

Windows, as desired

Door

Pea gravel

Wood-chip mix for surface

4' level

Shingles and plywood for roof

Posts frame out a deck that holds an L-shaped cabin. Reclaimed wood siding is affixed directly to the posts. The deck creates a second play space below, underneath the house.

SUNSET CONTRIBUTING EDITOR
PETER O. WHITELEY ON

reclaimed materials

>> Reusing wood, windows, and doors adds a weathered, vintage feel to new buildings. Be sure to test for lead in paint before installing reclaimed pieces. You can buy easy-to-use lead test kits at hardware and home improvement stores.

BUILDING THE PLAYHOUSE

❶ Set the Posts

Clear the site. Dig oversize post holes 2 feet deep or below frost level. Pour 5 inches of pea gravel into each hole for drainage. Use string lines to ensure support posts are in alignment. Stand 4 x 4 posts into each hole. Use a 4-foot level to ensure posts are plumb in both directions. Stake securely. Posts need to be higher than the overall finished height of the structure. Pour concrete mix around each post. After pouring concrete, recheck that posts remain plumb. Let cure. If you live in a wet or freezing climate, consult a local builder for an alternative method of setting posts that won't encourage rot.

❷ Build the Deck

Determine height of deck. Using lag bolts, attach 2 x 6 boards to the outside of the 4 x 4 posts, creating a level box. Install 2 x 6 joists spaced 16 inches apart using joist hangers for support. Once the frame is secure, add decking perpendicular to the floor frame using deck screws.

❸ Build the Stairs

Use 2 x 10s with angled cuts for stringers. Use lag bolts to affix the stringers to insides of posts. Affix cleats for treads. Cleats are 2 x 4s screwed to stringers level to the ground and sides. The distance from the top of one cleat to the top of the next cleat is approximately 8 vertical inches. Attach 2 x 6 treads on top of cleats.

❹ Construct the Roof

Frame roof with 2 x 6 boards using deck screws, attaching one to the outside of each post and angling the roof for drainage. Install roof joists 16 inches apart with 2 x 6s perpendicular to the roof slope, starting high to low. (These will be easy square cuts.) Use joist hangers for support. Cover the portion of the cabin roof to be finished with shingles with plywood sheeting. Attach corrugated plastic for the rest of the roof, affixing sheets to the rafters at an angle so water drains from the grooves. Use screws with neoprene washers to affix roof sheets.

❺ Build the Playhouse

Frame spaces for windows, entry door, and peek-a-boo door. Affix siding starting from the bottom; secure to posts. Overlap boards as you go up. Attach windows and doors with hinges.

❻ Add Siding on Lower Level

Space lower-level siding boards 2 inches apart to achieve this design's airy look. Attach to posts. Frame space for shutters if desired.

❼ Build the Railing

Use 2 x 4s for railing. Attach 1 x 1 rails 3 inches apart for balusters.

❽ Embellish

Leave openings for store windows, peek holes, or secret passages as you wish. Add mailbox, lucky horseshoes, or other items for charm.

A mailbox holds notes and special deliveries.

You'd never know you're being watched through this hidden peek hole.

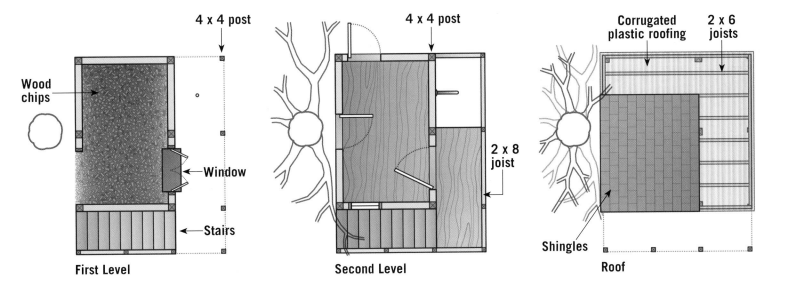

First Level

Second Level

Roof

cottage
cool

Rich Soenksen Design

As soon as they saw this property's backyard, the homeowners-to-be knew they'd found their dream house. They were certain their three daughters would love it. And after moving in, they began planning the perfect playhouse for the space. The cottage they created has supported hundreds of homework sessions, cookie tastings, and slumber parties—the generous loft sleeps four. The place was even once turned into a short-lived restaurant, serving up a memorable anniversary meal for the happy couple.

Design

Echoing the Craftsman styling of the main house, this playhouse has authentic domestic details in the casement windows, wood shingles, window boxes, board-and-batten gable siding, and deck porch. The oversize boards and posts add to the Craftsman look.

can I do this?

With a concrete tube foundation, sleeping loft, and trussless roof, this construction job requires expert skills. The assembly requires two to three people and will take several weekends.

DEGREE OF DIFFICULTY

1   2   3   4   **5**
        (difficult)

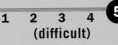

design lesson

>> In most places, you'll need a building permit for a project of this size. Check with your city office while you're still in the planning stages. Be sure to follow rules on setbacks and roof heights. You may want professional help in design and construction. The homeowners for this project worked with an architect and his design-and-build company.

WHAT YOU'LL NEED

4 x 4 skids

8 x 8 posts

2 x 6 joists

4 x 8 beams

2 x 8 boards

2 x 4s and 3 x 4s for studs and rafters

4 x 6 beams

Wood shingles

Boards and battens for siding

Joist hangers

Windows

Door

Paint

Rigid fiber building tubes for foundation

Concrete mix

Gravel

Roofing nails

Brackets for foundation

Rafter ties

BUILDING THE PLAYHOUSE

1 Set the Foundation

Clear the site. Mark the perimeter using string lines. Use stakes to identify spots for the 8 x 8 posts and cut rigid fiber tubes for the foundation to the desired length. Dig four post holes at least 2 feet deep or below the frost line and wide enough to fit the tubes. In each hole, pour a 6-inch layer of gravel. Center the tubes in each hole. The finished footings should extend out of the ground 2 to 6 inches. Check that the tubes are level. Carefully backfill around the tubes with gravel. Fill the inside of the tubes with concrete and top each footing with adjustable brackets. Recheck that each one is level. Let cure.

2 Construct the Floor

Affix a 4 x 8 beam to each adjustable bracket embedded in the poured concrete footings. The beams should run front to back, one on each side (extend beams beyond the front walls if you are building a deck as well). Place the beams in the brackets so that they stand 8 inches tall. Check for level and secure with bolts. Install joist hangers and 2 x 6 floor framing between the 4 x 8 beams, 16 inches on center, and cover with pre-primed plywood sheeting.

3 Build the Walls

Set 8 x 8 posts, then frame between them with 2 x 4 framing placed 16 inches on center. Factor in the height for the roof beams on each side wall and a support for the ridge beam on each gable wall. Frame the windows and door, then frame the loft as desired.

4 Assemble the Roof

Top both side walls with 4 x 6 timbers that extend beyond the playhouse frame to the front and back. After nailing a king post to the top of each gabled wall, hoist the ridge beam into place on top of the post, securing with rafter ties. Cut 3 x 4s at an angle for the rafters and affix to the ridge beam with joist hangers every 16 inches on center. Extend rafters over side walls 12 to 24 inches to create the Craftsman-style eve overhang.

LEFT: Without trusses, this playhouse has more sleeping space in the loft. The sizeable roof beam ensures sturdiness and adds a Craftsman touch. The loft is half the size of the floor, so there's room for homework below.

RIGHT: Floors and walls are painted white to keep the interior bright. The exposed studs serve as frames for art.

❺ Sheath the Walls

Nail plywood sheets to the wall exteriors. Install windows. Then cover the rafters with plywood sheets. For a shingle roof, begin with a line of starter shingles at the bottom and work upward, spacing shingles 1/8 to 1/4 inch apart using roofing nails. Stagger seams so they don't line up.

❻ Construct the Loft

Use 2 x 8s to frame the loft base, attaching to studs with joist hangers. Consider the desired loft ceiling height and adjust the floor accordingly. Secure the loft beam to the ridge beam and frame the loft walls. Frame the rest of the loft floor with 2 x 6s, affixing every 16 inches. Top with plywood sheets.

❼ Finish the Exterior

For exterior siding, begin with a line of starter shingles at the bottom of a wall. Work upward, spacing shingles 1/8 to 1/4 inch apart, affixing with roofing nails. Stagger seams so they don't line up. For upper-story board-and-batten siding, nail wide boards in place only along one edge, leaving at least a nail's width between boards. The battens will hold the other edge in place. Attach battens with nails that fit into the spaces between the wide boards. Paint boards and battens, and trim.

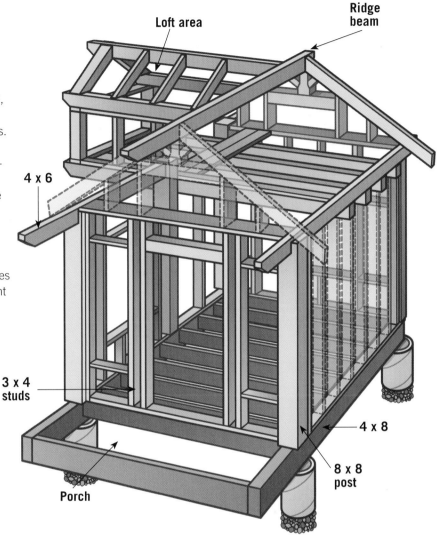

Loft area

Ridge beam

4 x 6

3 x 4 studs

4 x 8

8 x 8 post

Porch

creating a dutch door

» A half door adds many playful opportunities: store counter, puppet show, or simply a spot to lean and dream. To build one, select a solid-wood door that has a wide piece of wood going horizontally across the middle. Saw through this piece to cut the door in half, taking care to miss the doorknob hole. Sand the top thoroughly. Attach a stop to the outer edge of the upper door section to prevent the panels from swinging past each other. Affix a metal latch anchored on the lower door so you can lock the halves back into one piece.

Trisha Olson, Out-N-In

Wrap bamboo poles in colorful fabric and—voilá!—you have an instant, delightful retreat. Add cushions for a cozy base. This tent is an easy project for anyone not wanting to build a permanent structure, and it's perfect for a summer backyard campout.

Design

The designer sewed two layers of fabric together for this colorful fort. The exterior is weather-resistant Sunbrella fabric lined with striped linen for punch.

can I do this?

Simple assembly can be completed in half an hour. To customize, sew fabric panels together.

DEGREE OF DIFFICULTY

1 **2*** 3 4 5
(moderate)

*If sewing your own covering

WHAT YOU'LL NEED

Five 10' bamboo poles, 2" diameter

Sisal rope

Camping tarp

Blanket big enough to wrap around poles

Steel safety pins

Air mattress and pillows if desired

CONSTRUCTING THE TENT

❶ Assemble the Frame

Measure an 81-by-59-inch rectangle on the ground. Place four bamboo poles upright, one at each corner. Place a fifth pole between the two back poles for stability. Tether the poles with sisal rope. Spread the camping tarp beneath the bamboo frame.

❷ Make the Walls

Wrap the blanket around the frame, covering it completely so that the ends meet in the front. Secure at the top front with the safety pins.

❸ Add Coziness

Put the mattress inside the tent and inflate. Add pillows and blankets as desired.

LEFT: You can accomplish something similar without having to sew. This example uses shorter, lighter poles and a bed sheet.

RIGHT: Playhouses can be made with fabric as well. This simple structure is held up with tent framing. Cut out holes for windows and doors and use paint to add a theme.

room with
a view

TreeHouse Workshop

The dream of a 9-year-old boy, this treehouse is eight feet off the ground and supported by Douglas fir trees. It offers a nice view of trails leading to the house and neighbors' homes. Located 12 feet from the house's back deck, it's a getaway that feels a world away even though it isn't so far from home.

Design

Constructed professionally by the TreeHouse Workshop and following the boy's initial vision, the lookout has tall thin windows and a heavy door. Before getting started, the family called an arborist to remove dead branches and to thin the trees to increase stability.

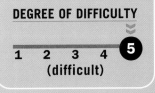

can I do this?

This is a challenging project, as the treehouse's complexity varies somewhat with the location of the supporting trees. This job requires a team of at least three, and building the support structure is not a job for children.

DEGREE OF DIFFICULTY

1   2   3   4   **5**
(difficult)

WHAT YOU'LL NEED

Two nave brackets

4 x 8 Douglas fir beams

2 x 6 Douglas fir joists

2 x 4 Douglas fir for deck

2 x 4s for bracket template, studs, window and door frames

2 x 6s for framing

Pressure-treated decking

1 x 8 cedar for deck railing

2 x 6 cedar for deck

2 x 4 cedar for deck trim

4 x 4s for posts and framing

1 x 10 for siding

Construction adhesive

Exterior plywood

Metal roofing

Lag bolts

Galvanized bolts with nuts and malleable iron washers

Ceramic-coated deck screws

Deck screws

Roofing screws

Ridge cap

Windows

Door

BUILDING THE SUPPORT STRUCTURE

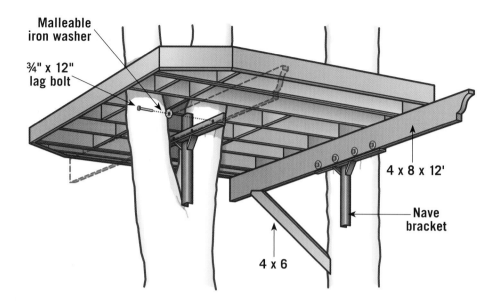

Malleable
iron washer

¾" x 12"
lag bolt

4 x 8 x 12'

Nave
bracket

4 x 6

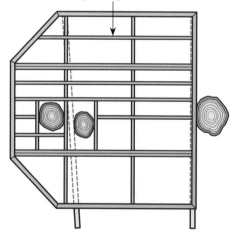

2 x 6
joist system

❶ Design the Nave Bracket

The key element in building a treehouse is attaching it to the tree or trees so the house is supported but doesn't damage the tree. The easiest way to achieve this is to order custom T-shape supports from a metal fabricator or welding shop. The TreeHouse Workshop refers to these pieces as nave brackets. To make a template for the nave bracket fabricator, strap a 40-inch-long 2 x 4 along the central axis of the trunk. Then level and screw on a 2 x 4 crosspiece at the height of the lowest edge of the treehouse deck structure.

❷ The Finished Nave Bracket

The vertical piece is a length of 3-inch steel channel. The crosspiece is a length of 3-inch angle iron. Both are ³/₁₆ inch thick. These pieces are welded into a cross, arranged so that the upper section does not project beyond the height of the deck. Steel triangles welded to the main pieces provide reinforcement. A ¾-inch hole at each end of the vertical piece and four holes along the crosspiece allow the fitting to be screwed to the tree and to the deck supports.

❸ Drill Pilot Holes

After establishing one tree as a reference point, strap a nave bracket into place and drill pilot holes for the two ¾-inch galvanized lag screws that will secure the metal to the tree. Use a long auger bit in a half-inch drill equipped with handles, available from tool-rental companies. Or, to do the job using homeowner-scale tools: Drill down as far as possible with a spade bit, then add a bit extension and continue drilling to the depth needed for the bolts.

❹ Affix the Second Nave Bracket

Strap a 2 x 4 to the bottom of the first bracket and extend the wood to the other tree. Using a level, fine-tune the position of the 2 x 4. Temporarily screw it into place. Repeat this process with a second 2 x 4 on the other side of the trees. With a helper or two, hoist the second nave bracket and bolt it into place.

❺ Bolt Beams to Brackets

With both nave brackets attached, bolt on one of the 4 x 8 support beams. The shelf created by the angle iron makes this step easy as long as all the holes line up. The malleable iron washers provide more bearing surface than ordinary flat washers.

❻ Frame the Deck

Made of 2 x 6 Douglas fir, the deck rim is more secure with ceramic-coated deck screws. When you're working on a ladder, a drill gives you more control than a hammer does, and parts stay aligned better.

❼ Brace Framing to Trees

Before adding the rest of the framing, install two diagonal braces to help shift the tree-house's weight back to the trees. Figuring out where to cut the braces is tricky because the top must be inset slightly into the beam, while the base needs to fit perfectly flush with the bark. To create a template for the top cut of the diagonal brace, snap a chalk line onto stiff paper and then copy the shape onto the beam.

❽ Bolt the Brace to Trees

The lower edge of the diagonal brace requires only a simple angle cut and perhaps a little paring of the bark so there's a flat place for the end to rest. Shallow cuts into a small section of bark won't harm the tree. To keep the tree's moisture from wicking into the diagonal brace, slip a piece of mudsill gasket material into the joint and then attach the brace to the tree with a 12-inch galvanized lag bolt.

BUILDING THE DECK AND TREEHOUSE

Plan the work of building the treehouse so that you can stand on the ground or on the platform whenever possible. Working on a ladder is not only more dangerous, it's also more time-consuming and harder on your body.

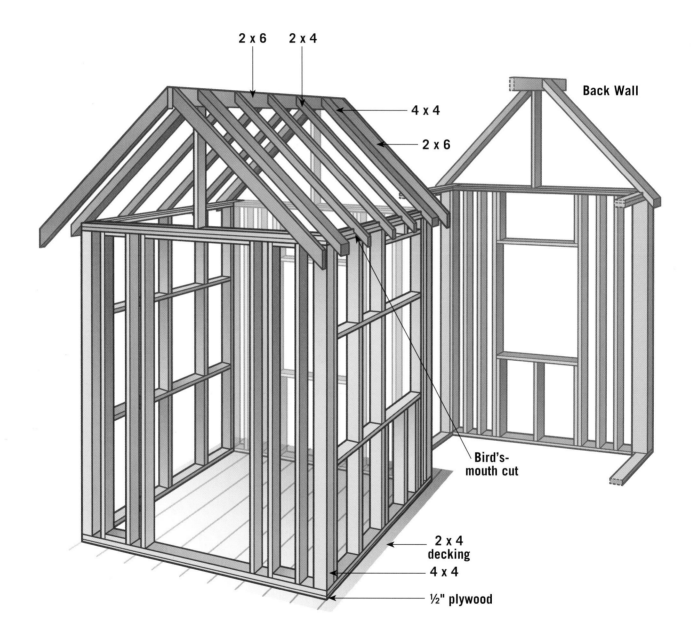

2 x 6
2 x 4
4 x 4
2 x 6
Back Wall
Bird's-mouth cut
2 x 4 decking
4 x 4
½" plywood

❶ Install the Floor

After installing a network of 2 x 6 joists spaced about 16 inches apart, screw on 2 x 6 deck boards as flooring for the outdoor areas and as a subfloor for the interior.

❷ Glue Interior Subfloor

A liberal zigzag of construction adhesive along the perimeter of the floor, and at regular spots in the middle, seals the plywood floor to the decking and keeps rainwater out. The decking alone would be strong enough for a treehouse floor, but the addition of plywood allows for interior carpeting.

❸ Frame the Walls

Frame the first wall on the ground and then lift it onto the platform, where you can install the window. It's easiest to build everything on the ground, but the weight can become too much for a few people to lift without the help of pulleys and ropes. Doing the work partly on the ground and partly on the platform is the easiest solution.

❹ Attach the Siding

The treehouse's two side walls nearly abut the trees. Here the board-and-batten siding and exterior window trim were installed before the walls were fixed in place.

❺ Raise the Rafters

After nailing a king post to the top of each gabled wall, hoist the ridge beam into place on top of the posts and nail on the rafters. Notches in the rafters, called "bird's-mouth" cuts, provide secure footing against the top plate. Using metal rafter ties instead would simplify this step.

❻ Build the Deck Rails

For the deck railing, builders used branches trimmed from the lot's fir trees and supplemented them with cedar branches, also from the property. Because branches are rarely straight, the TreeHouse Workshop crew built a jig that allows each piece to settle into its natural alignment. The jig also makes it easy to cut each piece exactly to length. A screw through each end secures the branch pieces to the railing frame. For a sturdy railing, use only sound branches that are at least 1½ inches in diameter and space them 3 inches apart.

clatter-bridge entry

TreeHouse Workshop

L inking the treehouse to the family's deck, this bridge adds a fantastic entry to the treehouse. And it makes a fabulous sound every time there's a visitor. Manila rope serves as handrails.

Because this bridge is not very high off the ground, and because it was designed for an older child, the rope rail is sufficient. For more security, you could string a second rope rail lower down and then weave it diagonally to create netting.

LEFT: The bridge rests on galvanized chains and carriage bolts threaded through the links to secure the planks.

Design

To get up to the level of the treehouse floor, the builders installed a ladder at one end of the bridge and diagonal braces serve as a handrail for the ladder. They also bolster the bridge's support posts, which are set into concrete. Cutouts in the decking allow the diagonal braces to run underneath the deck and tie into its support structure. On the treehouse end, the chains pass through holes in the rim joist of the deck and are bolted to the next joist. Given all the bouncing on the bridge, strong connections at both ends are very important.

can I do this?

The bridge's essential element is stability. Be sure your connections are solid so that the structure can withstand the swinging of the bridge. It's helpful but not essential to have an assistant in hanging the bridge.

DEGREE OF DIFFICULTY

1   2   **3**   4   5
(moderate)

WHAT YOU'LL NEED

Pressure-treated 4 x 4 posts

2 x 12 boards

Manila rope, 1½" thick

Lag bolts

Galvanized chains

Carriage bolts

Concrete mix

❶ Set the Posts

Clear the site. Dig oversize postholes 2 feet deep or below frost level. Pour 5 inches of pea gravel into each hole for drainage. String lines to ensure support poles are in alignment. Stand one post into each hole. Use a 4-foot level to ensure the posts are plumb in both directions. Stake securely. Pour mixed concrete around each post. After pouring the concrete, recheck that the posts remain plumb. Let cure.

❷ Build the Bridge

When measuring lengths of galvanized chains to connect the posts, leave enough slack for the bridge to arch. Drill holes into rim joists (at either end of the bridge attachments) large enough to fit galvanized chain, then thread the chain through drilled holes. Anchor securely with lag bolts. Thread carriage bolts ½-inch thick through every other link of each of the two galvanized chains, two bolts per 2 x 12 plank. Affix planks perpendicular to the chains.

❸ Attach the Handrails

Attach Manila rope to each end, affixing to posts. You can drill through the posts if desired. Be sure the ropes are attached securely at each end, and do not leave excessive slack. Attach ropes securely to deck handrails on each side.

simple
swing

A backyard swing promises old-fashioned fun and can do the job whether the mood is energetic and high swinging or contemplative and lazy. Another bonus: A swing's entertainment life span is long, from childhood through the days when those children have children of their own.

Design

S-hooks drilled through a branch provide a longer-lasting swing support system than looping rope. And they are actually easier on the tree. These swing supports are braced by curved metal panels to further protect the bark. For each attachment point, the builder wove a loop, known as an eye splice, to increase durability. The swing seat is a recycled-tire design.

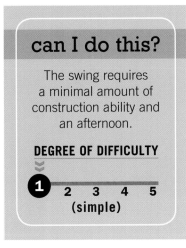

can I do this?

The swing requires a minimal amount of construction ability and an afternoon.

DEGREE OF DIFFICULTY

1 2 3 4 5
(simple)

WHAT YOU'LL NEED

Polyester rope, 1" thick

Swing seat

S hooks, long enough to extend through the tree branch

Curved metal plates for bracing

Locking washers and nuts

Metal thimbles sized for 1" rope

Wire

15 mm spring-shaped plastic sheathing for rope

S-hook tool

Constructing the Swing

❶ Drill Holes

Use common sense in making sure the rope is not hung too close to the tree's trunk or any surrounding objects, and that the swing is not too close to the ground, so your child can swing freely and safely. Measure and drill holes through the branch. Be sure the branch and tree are sturdy enough to handle the weight of the swing and the heaviest child who will use it. Consult an arborist if you are unsure.

❷ Test the Hardware

Each drilled hole should be through the thickest parts of the branch. Test that the S hooks fit through the branch.

❸ Affix the Hardware

Fasten the hooks with curved metal braces, nuts, washers, and locking washers. The metal braces distribute the weight of the swing to protect the branch from wear.

SUNSET CONTRIBUTING EDITOR
PETER O. WHITELEY ON

maintenance

>> Check swing equipment regularly. S-hooks, caribiners, thimbles, and other metal parts that rub can wear out and need to be replaced periodically.

④ Make an Eye Splice

Cut rope to length, leaving some extra. Make an eye splice (see instructions at right). Lash the ends with wire for added security and cover with spring-shaped plastic sheathing. Make an eye splice for the other piece of rope. Once the eye splices are finished, attach them to each S-hook. Check that your positioning is satisfactory before using the S-hook tool to close the hooks securely. Affix the seat by wrapping the rope around the seat arms and cover the ends with plastic sheathing.

Eye Splice Details

1 Unravel 4 inches at one end of the rope. Create an egg-sized loop. Tuck one unraveled strand under the rope at the base of the loop.

2 Thread a second strand under the next strand in the rope.

3 Flip the eye over and tuck the third strand under the remaining rope strand. Complete the eye by repeating the first three steps twice more.

4 Trim the ends.

5 Reinforce the eye with a spliced metal thimble.

little space,
big play

A play set offers lots of choices for lots of kids: A slide and a sandbox delight youngsters, while swings and a climbing net engage kids as they get older. The lookout platform inspires fantasy games and group play. And there's room for all of this at once!

Design

Choose the size of your play set and its location based on your yard's specifics. The homeowners here had limited room, so they selected a set that packs in a lot of activity in a 14-by-13-foot space. They chose to situate the set so that it could be seen from the house, and they shifted the slide to the side opposite what was called for in the kit's plans to allow for adequate landing space. A simple customization like this is easy to accomplish. Kits typically include all hardware and precut pieces of wood except the main 4 x 4 posts and beams.

can I do this?

Play sets involve some basic construction tasks for assembly. Depending on the structure's size, you may need an assistant to help position the larger pieces.

DEGREE OF DIFFICULTY

1   2   **3**   4   5
(moderate)

WHAT YOU'LL NEED

Play set kit, including hardware

4 x 4 posts and beams

Rubber mallet

Carpenter's square

Cordless drill

Work gloves

Pliers

Level

Safety glasses and dust mask

Tape measure

Hammer

Socket wrench set

Building the Play Set

❶ Assemble the Frames

Check kit inventory and make sure you have all the parts. Begin by attaching interlocking brackets to 4 x 4 posts. Measure the spacing of the brackets carefully and examine them to ensure you're using the right ones. Check that the holes line up before securing the brackets with 2-inch lag screws. The vertical posts and horizontal beams create two frames that form the skeleton of the play set. Attach the lower and upper beams to the posts using a carpenter's square to ensure that they are at right angles to the posts.

❷ Connect the Frames

Use the kit-supplied 4 x 4s to connect the frames to each other and create the edges of the platform's floor. Have a helper push from the opposite side of the structure to stabilize as you install the lag screws through the bracket holes. The frame will get heavier as you build, so determine that the structure is exactly where you want it before installing the floor.

❸ Install the Floor

Attach the center floor joist, using a rubber mallet if necessary to tap it into position. Place the short floorboards at either end of the floor area, setting them parallel. Tap the boards into place and secure them with screws, including one through the center floor joist and two at each end. Secure the remaining floorboards.

❹ Affix the Rail Boards

Once the deck floor is constructed, you can use it to stand on while you build the rest of the structure. Use screws to attach horizontal rail boards first, then attach vertical pickets.

❺ Install the Swings

Working on the ground, mark and measure holes for the swing hangers. Drill holes and tap in the T nuts with a hammer. Lay out the 4 x 4 beams and align their edges with the edges of the frame bracket, bracket facing outward. Before securing the bracket completely with screws, lay out the 2 x 4 cross member to make sure it is positioned correctly. Flip the frame over to install the second bracket.

❻ Secure the Swing Beam

Attach the A-frame to the swing beam, using a mallet to tap the hex bolt in gradually before ratcheting securely. Make sure the tightened bolt is flush or nearly flush with the surrounding surface. Repeat with the second bracket and bolt hole. Lift the A-frame, tipping it upright so that the end of the swing beam lines up with the bracket installed on the beam above the platform. Double-check that it's level, then secure it with screws.

❼ Build the Climbing Wall

Construct the climbing wall on the ground, then place plastic rocks in positions to create climbing routes. Choose the route, then drill the holes for bolts and T nuts. Make sure none of the rocks are positioned too close to the edges of the wall.

❽ Finish the Details

Affix handles on posts to aid in conquering the climbing wall. Install the periscope so that it offers a nice view. The steering wheel can go on the back wall of the lookout platform. The oilcloth fabric topping the platform offers shade.

spectacular perch

This two-story lookout tower and swing set in Southern California appeals to adults as well as children. The entire family likes to gather here after a cookout. With the swing seating plus Adirondack chairs, there's a perch for everyone. The view from above is of a neighboring apple orchard and vegetable garden.

Design

The stone-sheathed concrete columns supporting the platform posts are attractive and ensure the structure can hold many visitors. Stone and other natural details in the design pair well with the native plant garden. The high platform for the tower provides roomy and shaded space below so adults can comfortably keep close watch. Generous cushioning at the base is needed for a slide of this height.

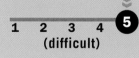

can I do this?

The height of the platform makes this a two- or three-person job. Hip-roof construction requires expert carpentry skills. Building and facing columns require expert masonry skills. You will likely require professional assistance. The homeowner who constructed this is a landscape architect.

DEGREE OF DIFFICULTY

1   2   3   4   **5**
(difficult)

WHAT YOU'LL NEED

8 x 8 support posts

4 x 8s and 4 x 10s for beams

4 x 8s for rafters

2 x 6s for decking

2 x 4s for rails and 2 x 6s for top rails

2 x 2s for balusters

Concrete blocks: 8 x 8 x 16 and 16 x 8 x 16

String line

Bricks

Stone

Slide

Swings

Bench swing

Rope or chain link for swings and rope for handrail

Lag bolts and machine bolts

Joist hangers

Deck screws

Veneer ties

Builder's felt

Concrete mix

Mortar mix

Angle-iron brackets

Pea gravel

Mulch or mats for landing areas

4' level

Nail plate connectors

Wood shingles

Jigsaw

Framer's square

Trowel

Eye bolts

Pan-head screws

Roofing nails

Rebar

4" adjustable post bases

Building the Tower and Swing Set

❶ Construct the Tower Columns

Clear the site. Mark and level the spaces for the concrete columns, excavating for the concrete footings 12 inches or per local codes. Pour the concrete footings with rebar set into the concrete for support. Four pieces of rebar should extend from the footing up to the top of each column. Build columns around the rebar, using two layers of 8 x 8 x 16 concrete blocks followed by 16 x 8 x 16 blocks. Arrange the concrete pier block columns with gradual steps inward to create a Craftsman-style "elephant leg" or tapered look. Build one column at a time, using mortar between blocks and then filling all blocks with mortar for added stability. Use horizontal rebar ties 32 inches on center as you go to tie the blocks together. Repeat laying blocks until the column is at the desired height. Set blocks for the remaining three posts, using string lines to ensure they are all level and square. Let cure.

❷ Set the Posts

Install adjustable brackets at the top of each concrete block tower column. Affix the 8 x 8 posts, using string lines to ensure the posts are in alignment. Use a 4-foot level to check that they are level and plumb. On the other side of the structure, mark the location for the swing post. Dig an oversize posthole 24 inches deep or below frost level. Pour 3 inches of pea gravel into the hole for drainage. This builder wrapped the bottom of the post with builder's felt to prevent rot. Drop the post into the hole. Use a level to ensure it's plumb in both directions. Stake securely. Pour mixed concrete around the post. After pouring, recheck that the post remains plumb. Let cure. Once the swing post is secure, face it with mortared 8 x 16 x 16 concrete blocks, using veneer ties to secure the blocks to the post every 12 inches on center.

❸ Build the Deck and Swing Frame

Mark tower posts for the height of the deck. Use a jigsaw to create decorative corbel edging on the beams. Using machine bolts, attach 4 x 10 beams to the inside and outside of the 8 x 8 posts, creating a level box. Affix the front beam to the swing post using machine bolts. Install 4 x 8 joists across the 4 x 10 support beams. Inset into the 4 x 10 beam 1 inch and secure with angle-iron brackets. Install the rest of the joists using joist hangers. Add decking on top using deck screws.

❹ Build the Ladder

Use 2 x 10s with angled cuts to form the stringers. Use lag screws to affix the stringers to the platform. Affix cleats for treads; cleats are made of 2 x 4s screwed to the stringers level to the ground and sides. The distance from the top of each cleat to the top of the next cleat is approximately 8 vertical inches. Attach 2 x 6 treads on top of cleats. Use rope for handrails, affixing securely with eye bolts. Do not leave excessive slack in the rope.

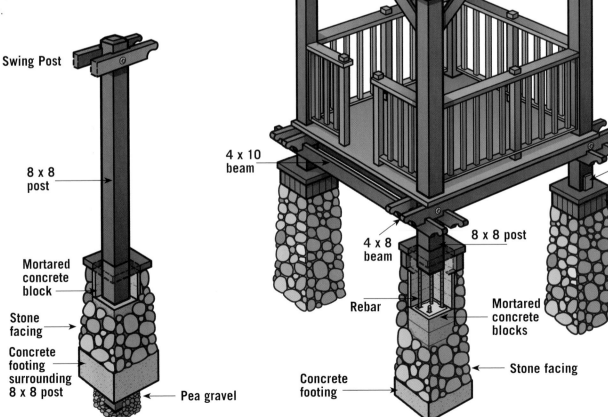

Lookout Tower

Swing Post

8 x 8 post

Mortared concrete block

Stone facing

Concrete footing surrounding 8 x 8 post

Pea gravel

4 x 10 beam

4 x 8 beam

Rebar

Concrete footing

8 x 8 post

Adjustable bracket

Brick

Mortared concrete blocks

Stone facing

❺ Construct the Hip Roof and Railing

Consult a contractor or roofing manual to frame and build the roof. This example was made of 3 x 10 girders attached to each post, and it's finished with wood shingles on top. Use 2 x 6s for the railing. Attach 2 x 2 rails 4 inches apart for balusters.

❻ Face the Columns with Stone

Use a pen to mark the dimensions of the column faces on plywood sheets on the ground. Lay out the pattern for the stone facing. Make cuts as necessary to fit the pattern. Mist a concrete pier block column with water and use a straight trowel to apply a ¼-inch-thick coat of type S or N mortar. Coat one side of the column at a time. Starting at the bottom, transfer stones from the plywood pattern to the wall. Press each stone into the mortar. The stone should be difficult to pull off; if it doesn't stick adequately, back-butter it with additional mortar. The builder also used veneer ties to help tie the stone and setting mortar back into the column structure. Avoid moving stones once the mortar has begun to harden. Use small stones in the gaps to brace if necessary. Move up the column. As soon as possible, wipe off any mortar that gets on the stone facing.

❼ Top the Columns

Dry-lay bricks around the top of each column, using dowels as spacers for mortar. Cut bricks as needed to fit around the wood posts. Remove the bricks, then work on one column at a time. Spread a layer of mortar on top of a stone-faced column and place the first brick. Repeat to create the desired pattern, buttering each brick end as you go. Use a trowel to slice off any mortar that squeezes out, and promptly wipe off any mortar that gets on the bricks. Once the mortar has hardened, use a mortar bag or small pointed trowel to fill the joints. Let cure.

❽ Attach the Swings and Slide

Attach the swings and slide according to the manufacturer's directions. Allow 14 feet of clearance at the base of the slide, and be sure there's adequate cushioning. If desired, attach a platform bench swing on the platform to the hip jacks in the roofing structure using eye bolts, making sure the swing hangs level from the angled rafters.

LEFT: At the corners, use a circular saw with a masonry blade to cut channels in the tops of the blocks. Bend a piece of rebar to fit in the channel, fill the cells with mortar, and set the rebar in the mortar. Do this every other course to tie the corners together.

RIGHT: Once the mortar has hardened, use a mortar bag or small pointed trowel to fill the joints. Overfill all gaps slightly. Wait until the mortar is stiff enough to hold a thumbprint before using a metal striking tool to wipe away excess. Let cure.

portable
sandbox

Carina Schott, Nonchalant
Mom Fashion Design

Made from reclaimed wood, this design's innovation is in its mobility: It's a sandbox on wheels! The design is perfect for a deck and a sunny day and can be rolled into protected territory when not in use.

Design

Tiny holes in the plywood base allow for drainage. Without them, the wood frame would bog down and eventually rot. But make the holes as small as possible, or sand will trickle out, leaving a trail marking everywhere the sandbox has traveled.

WHAT YOU'LL NEED

1 x 6 boards, preferably cedar

4 x 4 posts, preferably cedar

1 x 2 strips

1½" plywood sheet, pressure treated

5" urethane-on-iron industrial-grade casters

Water-based sealer

L brackets

Play sand

Stainless-steel screws

can I do this?

Assembly requires basic carpentry skills and a few hours. Hoisting the sand bags takes strength.

DEGREE OF DIFFICULTY

1   **2**   3   4   5
(moderate)

Building the Sandbox

❶ Weatherproof the Wood

Coat the plywood sheet and boards with a water-based sealer. Let them dry.

❷ Build the Frame

Drill a dozen or more very small holes into the plywood sheet, spacing them randomly, for drainage. Affix 4 x 4 posts at each corner of the plywood sheet using stainless-steel screws. About 12 inches in from one corner, affix a 1 x 2 across the plywood sheet using screws. Be sure the screws don't poke through. Repeat 12 inches farther in with another 1 x 2 laid parallel. Affix a third 1 x 2 for structural support. Affix 1 x 6 boards along each edge, creating a box. Attach 1 x 2 braces to the side boards with L brackets.

❸ Attach the Wheels

Attach casters to the underside of the posts using screws.

❹ Fill with Sand

Flip the sandbox over, position it, and fill it with clean sand graded for play. Once the box is filled, it will be much heavier and more difficult to move.

SUNSET CONTRIBUTING EDITOR PETER O. WHITELEY ON

wheels

This design uses industrial-grade casters to help with mobility, as a full sand box carries a lot of weight. Casters are graded on mobility and bearing load; these medium-grade ones can take loads of up to 1,200 pounds. The larger the casters, the easier the box will roll. You can add braking mechanisms to the casters if desired. Don't let toddlers play with wheels or brakes, as little fingers can get painfully pinched.

Peter O. Whiteley,
Sunset contributing editor

It's a delicious experience to take a shower in the open air. A fresh rinse-off in your backyard can transform a morning into a vacation. An added benefit: Runoff irrigates your garden. Be sure any soap you're using is made of ingredients that will not harm surrounding plants.

Design

This simple shower relies on an outdoor hose spigot for a quick (and cold) experience. A shallow gravel bed is adequate for drainage here, but grading the site and laying a deeper bed of gravel would prevent pooling if you wanted to linger in the shower. In that case, contact a plumber to add a warm-water option.

can I do this?

Assembling the screen requires basic carpentry skills. Putting together the plumbing pieces is simple.

DEGREE OF DIFFICULTY

1 **2** 3 4 5
(moderate)

WHAT YOU'LL NEED

Pea gravel

Concrete pavers

Corrugated metal roofing panels

2 x 4 redwood boards

Peeler-core log

Deck screws

Self-tapping metal screws

Water-based wood sealer

Nylon plumbing tape

Showerhead

Shower arm

½" elbows

½"-diameter pipes threaded at each end

½" threaded gate-valve faucet

Hose coupling, female hose to female swivel

C-shaped pipe hangers

Garden hose connected to exterior water spigot

Privacy Panels

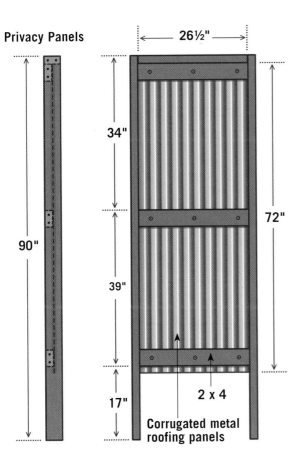

90"

26½"

34"

72"

39"

17"

2 x 4

Corrugated metal roofing panels

Top View

Concrete pavers

Plumbing Details

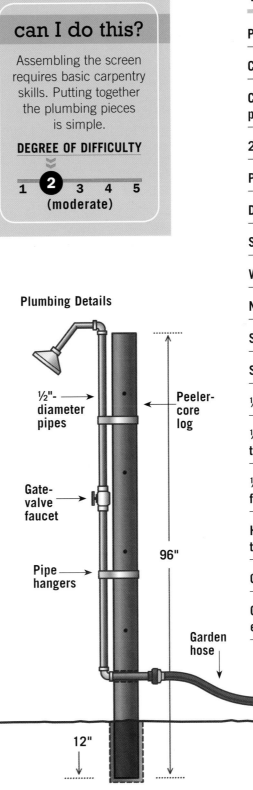

½"-diameter pipes

Peeler-core log

Gate-valve faucet

96"

Pipe hangers

Garden hose

12"

117

Constructing the Shower

① Prepare the Site and Wood

Coat all lumber with water-based sealer. Let dry. Clear the shower site. Excavate 2 inches and lay pea gravel. Top with several large concrete pavers to create a comfortable standing space, adjusting the pavers so they're level. Dig the center posthole 12 inches deep. Dig postholes for the wing walls 6 inches deep.

② Construct the Privacy Panels

Assemble the panels on the ground. Attach the top 2 x 4 piece to side pieces using weather-resistant screws. Attach the bottom 2 x 4 about 17 inches from the bottom of the side pieces. Affix the middle horizontal 2 x 4 lining up 34 inches from the top. Assemble the second panel, following the same measurements as with the first. Attach the corrugated metal panels to the wood frame with screws.

③ Plumb the Anchor Post

Center and drill a ¾-inch-diameter hole through the peeler-core log 78 inches from the top. Assemble the galvanized piping, faucet, and showerhead using nylon plumbing tape at each joint. Do not add the hose coupling at the end of the 8-inch bottom pipe yet. Slip the short leg of pipe through the hole, then center the pipe and faucet on the pole and secure with C-shaped pipe hangers. Add the hose coupling and then hook it up to the garden hose to test for leaks. Unfasten the hose.

④ Put It Together

Place the log pole so the faucet handle will project outward at a 45-degree angle between the wing walls. Adjust the position, then lightly tamp in soil around the base so the pole is secure. Set the wing walls square to each other with their legs 6 inches into the ground. Attach the wing walls to the center pole with 12-inch screws. Use a level to check that the walls are plumb before tamping and compacting the soil to secure the post and panels.

SUNSET MARKET EDITOR
JESS CHAMBERLAIN ON

brightening up

>> This plan called for panels of corrugated galvanized metal, but you could instead purchase clear, frosted, or colored panels of fiberglass roofing. For pops of color, try a waterproof fabric that's also weather-resistant.

Other Outdoor Shower Designs

For more privacy than the shower shown in this project, construct a fence and door. This example also features a raised platform with spaces between the slats so water can drain through the sand-laid brick below.

No time to build your own? Look for ready-made showers like this one that hook to a garden hose.

raised beds

Harvesting your own food is as satisfying as it is delicious, and this kitchen garden makes growing produce look gorgeous. The homeowners pride themselves on entertaining with meals for which everything is grown on site. Strawberries, corn, peaches, apples, and tomatoes are some of their favorite ingredients.

Design

Raised beds are the most efficient way to grow fabulous produce. The soil warms earlier in the spring and drains well. And without foot traffic, soil doesn't get compacted. Orient your beds to maximize sun exposure. Redwood or cedar boards are good wood choices, as they naturally resist rot. Finishing details such as batten trim connecting the framing boards and 2 x 8 caps that can be used as benches help create a polished look. These beds are 5 feet by 7 feet. Make sure when you design yours that you'll easily be able to reach the center of each bed from the edge.

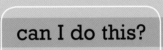

can I do this?

Assembling the beds requires basic carpentry skills. Having an assistant to help lift the frames will make the project easier.

DEGREE OF DIFFICULTY

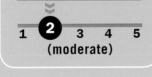

1 **2** 3 4 5
(moderate)

WHAT YOU'LL NEED

4 x 4 posts, preferably redwood or cedar

2 x 6 redwood panels for interior

1 x 6 horizontal siding, preferably redwood or cedar

2 x 8 redwood or cedar for caps

½" x 2 redwood or cedar trim

4 x 4 redwood or cedar for stringers

Lag screws and washers

Galvanized deck screws

Crushed aggregate

Concrete mix

6-mil plastic sheeting

Rake

¼" mesh hardware cloth

Garden shears

Planting mix

Water-based sealant

Building the Beds

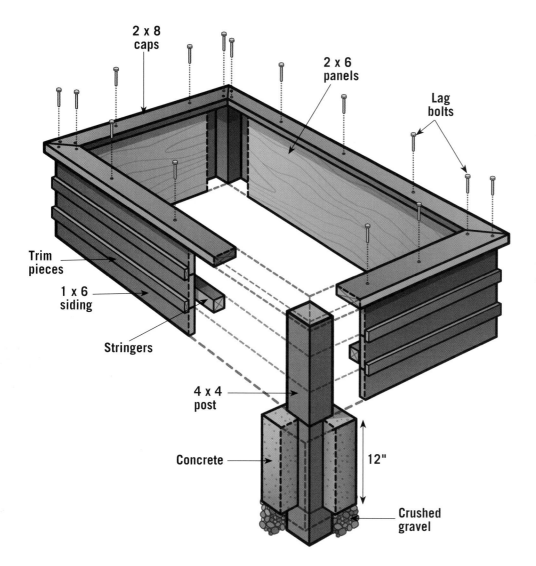

2 x 8 caps

2 x 6 panels

Lag bolts

Trim pieces

1 x 6 siding

Stringers

4 x 4 post

Concrete

12"

Crushed gravel

❶ Measure and Seal the Wood

Measure and cut the wood to size. The 4 x 4 posts should be the depth of the bed plus 12 inches to bury in the ground for support. Cut 2 x 4 stringers to fit horizontally between the posts. Coat all wood surfaces that will be exposed to the elements with a water-based sealant and let dry.

❷ Start the Frame

Build the beds upside down. Screw the 2 x 4 stringers to the 4 x 4 posts to create a frame. Then secure the 2 x 6 interior panels of redwood that will line the inside of the raised beds to the inside of the frame using galvanized deck screws.

❸ Set the Frame

With a helper, flip the bed right side up. Move it into position in your yard. Mark the corners and move the bed aside. Dig a 12-inch-deep hole for each post. Pour 3 inches of crushed aggregate into each hole for drainage. Set the frame into position and check to make sure it's level and plumb. Secure it with temporary stakes so it doesn't move. Pour mixed concrete around each post. After pouring the concrete, recheck that the raised bed is still plumb. Let the concrete cure.

❹ Finish the Frame

Use screws to attach 1 x 6 horizontal siding to the frame using galvanized deck screws. Sink the screw heads and miter-cut the corners. Then attach ½" x 2 trim pieces over the joints of the 1 x 6 siding. Place 2 x 8 redwood caps on top of each side of the planter so the edges hang just over the frame. Affix the caps to the posts and siding using lag screws and washers. Countersink to recess the heads.

❺ Line and Fill the Bed

Cover the interior 2 x 6 redwood panels with 6-mil plastic sheeting to prevent wood rot. Staple in place. Rake the bottom of the empty bed to level ground. Line the bed with hardware cloth to keep out pests, trimming the cloth with shears to fit around corner posts. Fill the bed with a planting mix of topsoil, compost, and potting soil so it is about 4 inches below the top of the bed frame. Rake the soil smooth.

LEFT: The ends of the posts are sticking up here, but once the frame is turned right side up, those posts will be set in the ground. For the project described on these pages, 2 x 6 redwood panels created the sides of the raised beds. Alternatively, you could use 2 x 6 boards, as shown in this photo.

RIGHT: Hardware cloth is optional, but it keeps pests from gaining access to your vegetables from underground.

feather
your nest

Chicken mania has swept the nation, and for good reason: Fresh eggs out-flavor store-bought ones by a heap of feathers. Chickens require minimal space to thrive and eat ticks and other insects. And keeping chickens teaches your kids to delight in other creatures.

Design

Moveable chicken coops are called chicken tractors. Farmers use them for maintaining fields and to aid in crop rotation. This scaled-down version suits a suburban "farm"—or at least a modest lawn and a few hens. The front end of the coop is lifted so the structure can roll at the back. Be careful when moving that chickens aren't disturbed.

can I do this?

Requiring a rectangular base and an A-frame top, this is a good starter project for a woodworker.

DEGREE OF DIFFICULTY

1 **2** 3 4 5
(moderate)

WHAT YOU'LL NEED

2 x 2s for frame

Plywood sheets

Circular saw

Corrugated plastic sheet

1" mesh netting

Wood screws

Hinges

Stapler

Scissors

Casters

Straw

Chicken wire

Wire clippers

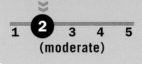

SUNSET CONTRIBUTOR
SAMANTHA SCHOECH ON
chicken contentment

》 This small coop would make two or three hens happy. Hens prefer to roost off the ground, 24 inches up if possible. The highest spot is their favorite place to sleep, so be sure to keep your nest box lower than the roosts. The truss piece here works great as a roost. Secure your coop at night from marauders such as raccoons and rats.

Building the Coop

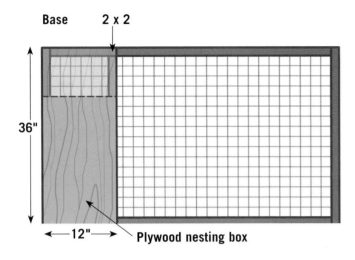

Base 2 x 2

36"

12" Plywood nesting box

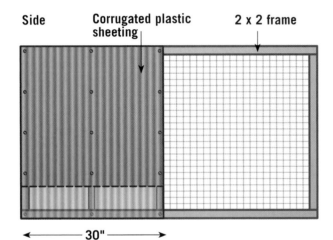

Side Corrugated plastic sheeting 2 x 2 frame

30"

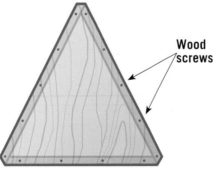

Door Back Panel

Wood screws

❶ Construct the Base and Sides

Measure and cut 2 x 2s to create a rectangular base. Attach using wood screws. Check that corners are square. Affix an additional 2 x 2 across the rectangle measuring 12 inches in from back edge. Cut plywood sheet to fit atop this 12" by 36" area and affix with wood screws. This will be for the nesting box. Measure two more similar rectangular frames out of 2 x 2s to create two panels for the A-frame. Affix 2 x 2 support boards across each panel similar to that on the base, but position them at 12 inches and 30 inches from the back edges.

Prop up the A-frame panels temporarily to measure angle cuts and the height for the 2 x 2 crosspiece. You want it to be 18 inches off the ground and level. Mark and cut both ends. An additional crosspiece could serve as a second roost spot. Lay one A-frame panel on the ground and affix the 2 x 2s with wood screws. Attach the second panel with wood screws. Tip the frame right side up. Cover the back of the panels with corrugated plastic that's 30 inches wide, attaching with screws. Cover the rest of the frame and base with chicken wire using a stapler.

❷ Attach the Back

Measure and cut a triangular plywood sheet to cover the back of the coop. Affix using wood screws. You can cut a simple egg-collecting door in the back of the sheet if desired. Cut it with a jigsaw just above the nesting box and attach hinges.

❸ Make the Nests

Build the nesting box using plywood pieces, 2 x 2s, and chicken wire. The box should be about 12 inches by 12 inches and 9 inches high. Affix securely to the platform floor at the back of the coop base. Line with straw. Hens can use the metal screen to climb to the upper roost.

❹ Construct the Door

Measure the front opening from inside the frame. Cut 2 x 2 lengths to create a triangular door. Attach the 2 x 2s using wood screws and use the stapler to cover the opening with mesh. Affix hinges on the outside at the upper and lower edges of the door frame. Lift the A-frame onto the base. Assemble it all along the perimeter of each panel, except for the doorway, using wood screws. The door folds all the way back. You can prop it open with a fabric or wire tie.

❺ Add Wheels

You may need to prop the coop on blocks or boards to attach the wheels. Add wheels at the back end of the coop, affixing them to the 2 x 2 base with screws.

canine
comfort

Peter O. Whiteley (designer)
and Jack Halloway (builder)

aturally, the beloved canine in your family should have her own cozy shelter. Designed for small to medium-size dogs, this board-and-batten structure offers privacy, shade, and a cushion for dog day naps.

Design

Board-and-batten siding and a lintel above the entryway add grandiosity to this simple box frame.

WHAT YOU'LL NEED

Plywood sheets

Circular saw

2 x 4s for floor and roof

2 x 2s

1 x 2 battens

Wood screws

Nails

Hammer

Jigsaw

Paint

Wood shingles

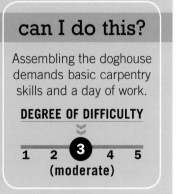

can I do this?

Assembling the doghouse demands basic carpentry skills and a day of work.

DEGREE OF DIFFICULTY

1   2   **3**   4   5
(moderate)

Building the Doghouse

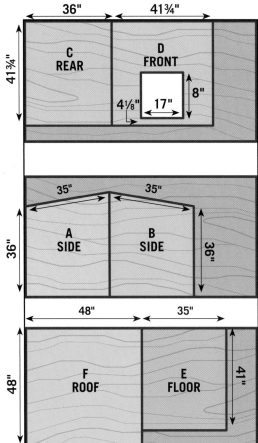

Plywood Cutout Templates

C REAR — 36"
D FRONT — 41¾", 41¾" (height)
8", 17", 4⅛"

A SIDE — 35", 36"
B SIDE — 35", 36"

F ROOF — 48"
E FLOOR — 35", 41", 48"

❶ Build the Floor

Before you begin, cut the plywood sides and panels for the rear, front, and roof (see illustration). Cut and screw four 2 x 4s to the underside of the floor panel so it sits off the ground. Mark the location of each 2 x 4 on the top of the plywood so you know where to place the screws.

❷ Add Reinforcements

Use a jigsaw to cut the entry door in a plywood panel. Reinforce each side-panel corner with one 2 x 2 that will run from the floor to ½ inch from the top edge. Screw side, front, and back panels to the floor.

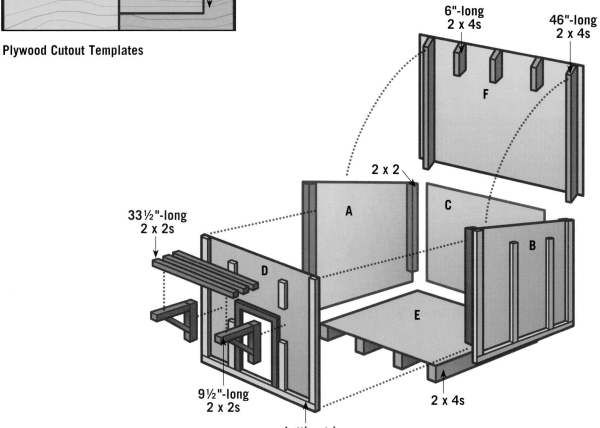

6"-long 2 x 4s

46"-long 2 x 4s

F

2 x 2

A

C

B

33½"-long 2 x 2s

D

E

9½"-long 2 x 2s

2 x 4s

Lattice trim

❸ Attach the Roof

Cut and screw 2 x 4s to the underside of a plywood panel to make the roof. The 2 x 4s on opposite ends will frame the sides of the structure, and the ones cut short will abut the front and back of the doghouse when the roof is put in place. Center the roof above the structure and use screws to attach the 2 x 4s to the side panels. The supporting 2 x 4s don't need to be screwed in, but they will prevent the roof from sliding back.

❹ Add the Battens

Use 1 x 2s to create decorative batten siding. The distance between the battens is 10 inches, from the outer edge of the first to the inner edge of the second. To avoid splitting battens, stagger placement of the nails.

❺ Nail Shingles to the Roof

Attach shingles with roofing nails, working from the back of the roof to the front.

❻ Construct the Lintel

Assemble the decorative lintel and triangular brackets out of 2 x 2s. Measure to make sure they will line up with the batten trim for a tailored, professional look and then attach with screws.

❼ Affix the Lintel

Center the decorative lintel over the entryway and attach it to the plywood with wood screws. Protect the structure using exterior water-based paint.

131

making
lemonade

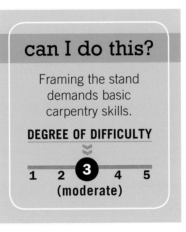

W hy not encourage entrepreneurship early on? It sure looks appealing here, and it might even pay off. If you end up with an adorable lemonade stand piled high with lemons...make lemonade!

Design

This family has taken the stand to city parades and local fairs. The plywood makes the frame heavy, so it's important to use large, high-quality wheels.

can I do this?

Framing the stand demands basic carpentry skills.

DEGREE OF DIFFICULTY

1   2   **3**   4   5
(moderate)

Alex Hodgkinson,
McCutcheon Construction

WHAT YOU'LL NEED

2 x 2s

1 x 2s

Plywood sheets

Jigsaw

Wood screws

Paint and chalkboard paint

Threaded metal rod

10" wheels

1" dowel

Fabric and upholstery tacks for awning

Drill

Sandpaper

Router

Nylon-threaded nuts and washers for wheels

Clear plastic panel

Building the Stand

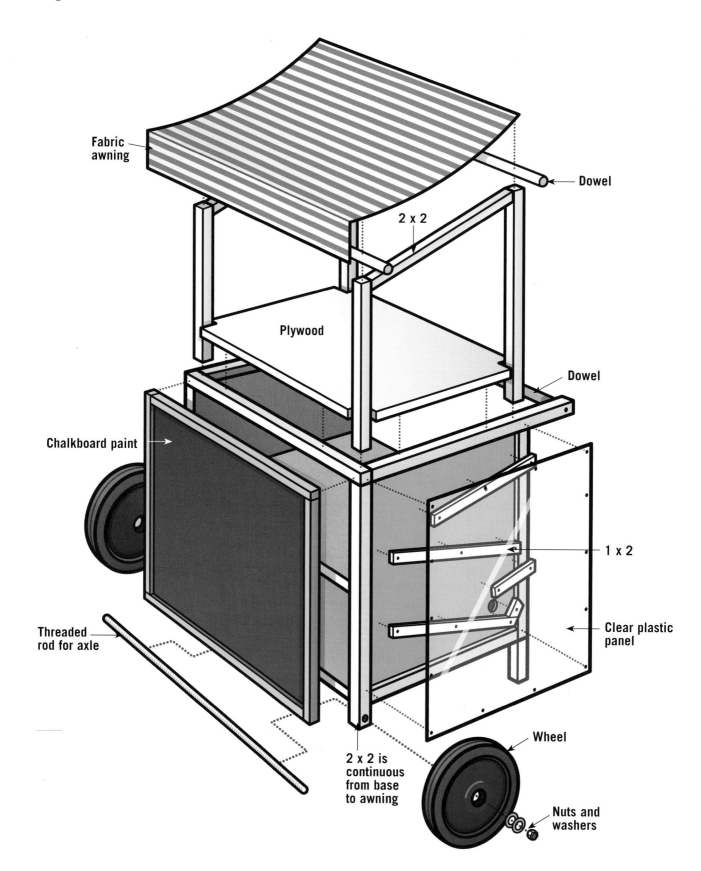

Fabric awning

Dowel

2 x 2

Plywood

Dowel

Chalkboard paint

1 x 2

Threaded rod for axle

Clear plastic panel

2 x 2 is continuous from base to awning

Wheel

Nuts and washers

➊ Assemble the Frame

Measure 2 x 2s for the frame, adjusting the length to accommodate the wheel height in front. Working on the ground, build frames for the side panels using wood screws. Measure and cut plywood sheets for each side panel. Attach them on the inside of the 2 x 2 frames using screws. Connect the first two panels with 2 x 2 pieces at the base of the cart. At countertop height, the 2 x 2s extend past the back posts to become handles connected with a dowel. Attach the other two sides of the frame. Frame the 2 x 2 supports at the top of the posts too, making the back support higher than the front to create an angle for the fabric top.

➋ Attach the Wheels

Predrill holes for the wheels in the front 2 x 2 posts. Cut a threaded metal rod to size so it extends past the front posts. Thread it through, and affix wheels with nuts and washers.

➌ Add Top and Bottom

Cut plywood sheets to create a base shelf and the top of the cart. Use a jigsaw to cut notches around the 2 x 2 posts to create dado joints. Attach the plywood using wood screws, affixing the bottom piece first and then the top piece.

➍ Finish the Stand

Measure the distance between the two 2 x 2s that extend past the back of the stand, cut a dowel to size for the handle, drill pilot holes, then screw the 2 x 2s into the dowel to secure it. Paint the cart and let it dry, then paint the front panel with chalkboard paint. Affix the fabric awning to the top dowels with upholstery tacks.

Be sure to add a stopper piece that will prevent coins from getting stuck in the side panel.

➎ Add the Coin Drop

Use a jigsaw to cut a slot a bit wider than the diameter of a quarter in the front left corner of the stand's counter; this will be the start of the coin drop. Drill a hole on the side of the stand toward the bottom (see picture) a bit larger in diameter than a quarter and sand the edges smooth; this is where coins will drop into the base of the stand.

Router out a shallow coin-sized groove in a 1 x 2, cut the 1 x 2 into short pieces, and lightly nail the strips in place onto the side panel. Test that a coin rolls down smoothly, adjust as necessary, then nail the strips all the way into place. Purchase a panel of clear plastic cut to size, drill pilot holes, and screw the panel into the 2 x 2 frame.

Finishing the Look

Creating your backyard play space involves a lot of decisions. Choose your materials and construct wisely, and you'll enhance your backyard's comfort, safety, and playfulness. This chapter will help you select the right materials to maximize the function and the fun of your designs. And don't forget your primary goal—making the space your own. Add style in details that finish the look. You want your yard to bring you joy year-round and into the future, and you want it to reflect and nurture your family's style of play. Make it fun, make it work!

Let the games begin! Plan well to create a fun, dynamic play area that works for small spaces.

A small yard lives large, with room for play, entertaining, and plants.

W̲e ask a lot of our backyards. The right designs for your space are functional and safe while fostering play.

As you get started on your project, you have much to think through: the size of the area, the cost of materials and construction, and the ways the space will be used. Be sure to balance your kids' needs as well as your own. Consider sun exposure, clearance, landing surfaces,

elevation, and sight lines. While younger children need to be closer to adults, older children may want some privacy. Spaces that can serve double duty or evolve over time are helpful for maximizing your efforts. A playhouse can become a storage shed in the future, for example, or shade-tolerant plants can add greenery in the space under a slide. Think about how you and your family will use your backyard now, and years into the future.

138

Consider All Your Senses

Shade-tolerant plants screen for privacy and add green. The murmur of leaves creates quiet music for playhouse visitors.

Add Color Everywhere

Painted pink shutters and a giant poppy on the front door pick up on the pinks and greens in the surrounding landscape.

Nurture Plants and Kids

One raised bed here is for vegetables, the other for sand. The shed can store seeds, tools, and toys.

Come One, Come All

Invite wildlife into your garden and you'll add enormously to the potential for discovery. Bring beneficial animals in by planting flowers for humming-birds and butterflies. A water feature can attract many creatures.

building a playhouse

A custom-designed playhouse with eco style.

Y ou can build your backyard playhouse yourself, assemble one from a kit, or adapt a purchased shed or structure. Find your approach by spending some time examining your playhouse vision. Consider your construction skills, time available, and how much you want to spend on the project. How do you want to use your yard? How much space do you have? How distinctive do you want the playhouse to be? How long will your family be using it? Could it serve multiple functions, now or in the future?

CONSTRUCTION OPTIONS Consider these when building a playhouse yourself

Standard Stud Construction

This is the longest-lasting method. Build a skeleton from 2 x 4s or 2 x 3s. Cover the framing with roofing and siding.

1. Build the floor first, then frame the walls on it.

2. Assemble walls horizontally so you can drive nails through the base and top plates into studs. Install windows while walls are still horizontal.

3. Make side walls as long as the floor. End walls should be the width of the floor minus the thickness of the two side walls.

4. Prop up one side wall, nail it to the floor, and brace it diagonally so it stays upright. Then prop up an end wall and fasten it to the floor and to the side wall. Add the other two walls.

5. Build the roof in place. Start by tacking uprights to temporarily support a ridge beam. Install the ridge beam, then each pair of rafters.

Plywood Shell

This is more easily relocated than other designs.

1. Use ¾-inch plywood for floors. Walls and roof can be ⅜ inch or ½ inch thick.

2. Lay out walls. Plywood generally comes in 4 x 8 sheets. Trim the floor to fit within the wall dimensions.

3. Screws and nails don't hold well when driven into the end grain of plywood. Reinforce fasteners by adding a piece of solid wood (1 x 2 or larger) to the rear plywood piece for secure attachments.

4. For doors and window shutters, cut the plywood only along the hinge line of the openings. Stop and add hinges. Then cut out the rest of the opening.

Pole Building

This is the easiest, fastest construction method. Set posts into the ground and use them for both the foundation and the corner posts of the structure.

1. Set pressure-treated posts into the ground at least 2 feet deep or below the frost line. Secure with either concrete or sharp-edged gravel packed tight.

2. Bolt rim joists onto the posts to support the floor and the roof.

3. Add vertical wall framing where needed, including on both sides of doors and windows, and frame the roof.

4. Add roofing, siding, and trim.

Foundation

You don't need a full-scale foundation for your playhouse, but you do need to keep the floor dry and the siding off the ground. Keep wood away from direct ground contact, if possible. Any wood that does come in contact with the ground or concrete should be pressure-treated. Set the floor joists on pier blocks (left) or standard concrete blocks. Fastening the structure to the blocks isn't crucial, because the weight holds it in place.

Adapt Another Structure

A simple shed transformed into a playhouse has style galore with a brightly painted interior and cottagey decor. Prefab storage sheds can be retrofitted as playhouses. Shed kits include lumber and fasteners but not foundations. Add colorful details to individualize.

Assemble from a Kit

Distinctive details such as branch railings make this kit stand out. Kits are usually packaged with floor, wall, and roof sections ready to be screwed into place. Costs vary. Check whether prices include shipping, fasteners, and a foundation.

Build at Home

A woodsy fort designed to blend into its forested surroundings, this playhouse is a modern twist on a log cabin. The frame is a small rectangle, with natural wood siding positioned vertically for rustic charm.

Ultimate Playhouse

This play cottage has all the elements of a real house, including building plans. With wood siding, a metal roof, a foundation, stairway entry, and multipaned windows and doors, this site-specific project required professional assistance to build.

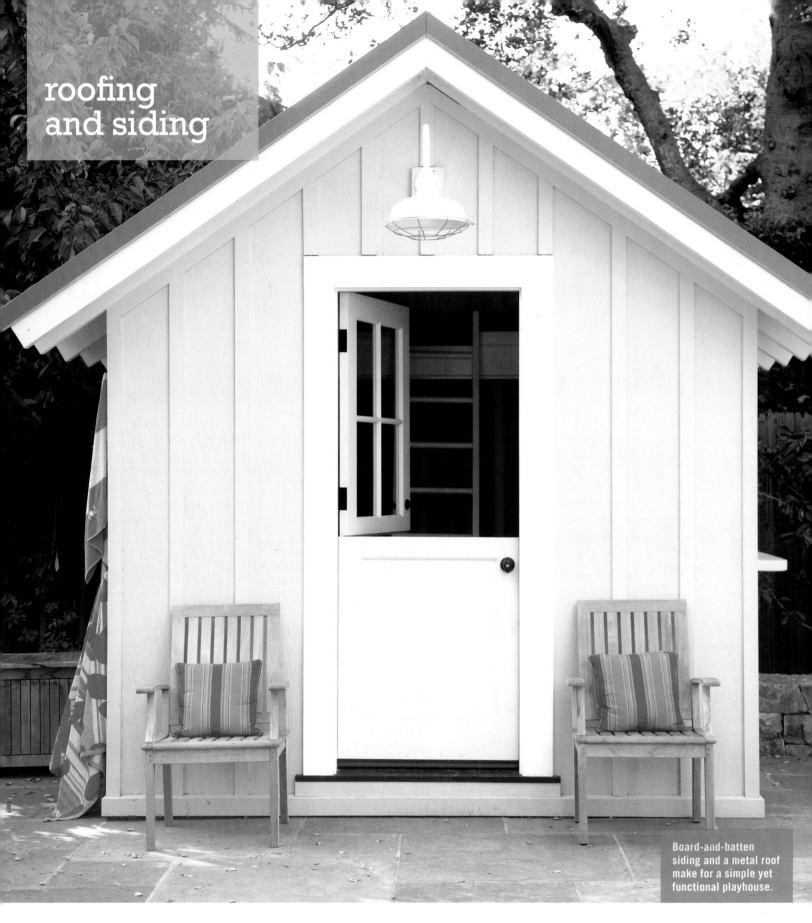

Board-and-batten siding and a metal roof make for a simple yet functional playhouse.

Make smart choices for the roof over your child's head and the walls around. Reusing materials is a good way to give your structure style and save cash—and it's also a good environmental move. Repurposing fence boards and installing simple corrugated metal roofing are additional ways to minimize expense.

Board-and-Batten Siding

Board-and-batten siding must be installed so the boards won't split when they expand and contract as humidity changes. Provide a generous overlap—at least ¾ inch for 4-inch boards and more for wider ones. Nail wide boards along one edge only, and leave at least a nail's width between fence boards or up to ½ inch with dry lumber. The battens will hold the other edge in place. Batten nails fit into the spaces between the wide boards.

Vertical boards absorb water along their bottom edge, increasing the risk of rot, so coat the ends liberally with an exterior-rated, water-resistant primer or polyurethane.

Another way to get this look for less money is to use fence boards for walls less than 6 feet tall. But the wood will probably be wet when you first buy it, which means you'll have to wait before painting it and it will shrink a little when it dries.

Metal Roofing

This roof material is inexpensive and easy to install. Screws with neoprene washers seal out the rain. Choose galvanized roofing for a rustic look or painted roofing for a more finished appearance. Use full-length pieces if possible. Otherwise, cut panels with a circular saw fitted with a special metal-cutting blade or a non-carbide blade set backward. Metal roofing flexes, so provide support to keep the blade from bending. When cutting, wear safety goggles to protect from metal shards. Also wear ear protectors and gloves. Install so the cut edges are hidden under the roof cap.

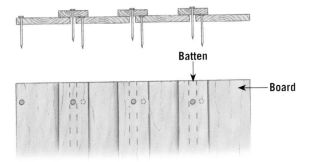

Batten

Board

Stripes, dots, flower accents, and lots of color give this place pizzazz.

Create a bright and lively playhouse inside. Colors energize a space; choose your child's favorite to anchor the palette. Lots of cushions and soft furnishings make a playhouse cozy for napping, floor games, and pillow fights. Downsize furniture in a smaller space and keep the scale consistent. Use baskets and bins for easy storage of games, toys, and extra blankets. Hooks are also invaluable. Accent with personal touches, such as your child's rock collection or designs with a favorite animal. Let your child help with the choices. Above all, make it a comfortable, personal space.

The Right Accessories

Beanbags are a childhood favorite. They're inexpensive and comfortable, and they soften playhouse corners. Plastic dishes make a playhouse picnic easy.

Artistic Expression

Celebrate your child's creativity with plenty of options. And decorate the playhouse with works created on the spot.

Inviting Nooks

Red and white stripes are crisp and appealing on this built-in daybed. The folding chairs and table echo the color pairing. They're also lightweight and easy to move.

Toys from Home

Stock your playhouse with tools and toys. Think through play activities your child likes and provide accessories with storage.

A Place to Crash

A nap nook is extra inviting with plenty of pillows. Natural fibers that can be machine washed are a good choice for fabrics.

Tools for Creativity

The appeal of lots of color applies to rugs as well as crayons. Keep kid favorites close at hand. Clear storage makes selection easier and helps maintain organization.

Color and Flexibility

A table and stools need not be ordinary. This lightweight and colorful furniture gives the whole place character.

Personal Accents

A fabulous turquoise play kitchen set pops next to purple furniture. The animal collection on the window shelf reveals a child's interests.

P lay sets can offer your children years of fun. The structures can include swings, slides, forts, decks, and climbing walls or nets. Choose stable, well-designed pieces that will work well for your yard and your child's age and interests. Young children enjoy small playhouses, slides, crawl-through holes, and tunnels. Older children like greater physical challenges and spaces that afford privacy.

This set has plenty of options: slides, a tunnel and sandbox, lookout platforms, and gymnastics rings.

SELECT A SET   What to consider

You can construct a play set yourself, buy precut plans and parts, or opt for a custom design.

Wood

» **For a wooden set,** look for 4 x 4 posts and 4 x 4 swing beams. Deck boards should be at least ¾ inch. Check that the wood is pressure-treated. All edges should be smoothed and corners rounded, particularly on railings and platforms.

Hardware

» **You'll find options** for residential and commercial-rated sets. Residential swing hangers carry up to 160 pounds on two chains. Commercial hangers hold 5,000 pounds. Choose the one that's best for the use the play set will get. Examine whether metal rubs against metal; look at swing hangers in particular. Hangers with nylon bushings last longer. Bronze bearings lubricated with oil sealed into the fitting are even better. Be careful of S hooks used to fasten chains or ropes, as S hooks can pinch skin and catch clothing if they are only partially bent shut.

Ropes and Chains

» **Investigate what load** the ropes or chains are designed to carry. Coated chain reduces the chance of pinched fingers. Polyester rope is softer to the touch than nylon, less stretchy, and more sun resistant. Rope ends should be fastened securely with a maximum slack allowance of a 5-inch circle for safety.

Stability

» **Check what age range** is specified on the play set. One described as suitable for children ages 2 to 5 may tip if older children use it. Metal braces and bolts with nuts should reinforce key joints, such as those between the swing beam and the play set legs. Connections that rely only on nails or screws are weak. Legs and braces should form triangles.

Swings

» **The higher the swing beam,** the larger the area of safety surfacing you need around it. Swings should be spaced at least 24 inches apart, and single-axis and multiple-axis swings should be separated.

Slides

» **Check slide construction.** Single-wall slides often need to have 2 x 4s bolted down the sides for support. Remember that preschoolers love slides but that the attraction often fades around kindergarten age.

swings

A solid branch can support many childhood afternoons.

Swings have an enduring appeal, and their draw can last through an entire childhood: Very young kids enjoy the thrill of bucket seats pushed gently by Mom or Dad. Then they graduate to gliders and tire swings. Even in elementary school and beyond, kids enjoy highfliers.

For Preschool Kids

A bucket seat is the safest for children ages 2 to 4. At this age children need supervision while swinging.

For Older Children

Swing seats made of lightweight rubber or plastic are preferable to heavier materials such as wood or metal. Whichever material you choose, make sure seat edges are smoothly finished or rounded.

Easy Construction

A tire swing hung from a sturdy tree branch is one of the simplest setups you can create in your backyard. Hardwood trees are best. Avoid fast-growing, soft-limbed varieties. Don't use steel-belted tires, as sharp cords might eventually appear.

safe landings

This simple wooden play set has a rope ladder and bucket swing, and it is supported by a concrete wall that doubles as a chalkboard. The rubber mat offers more cushioning for falls than the grass would.

It's impossible to eliminate all bruises and bumps from childhood. But minimize the risks around your play space by allowing for plenty of clearance for slides and swings and by providing a cushioned surface for landings. Even with the best planning and materials, you or another adult should supervise toddlers and preschoolers. As kids get older and more mature, your level of supervision will change.

Slides and Swings

If possible, allow 6 feet of clearance in all directions for slides. From the bottom of the slide, measure a safety zone equal to the height of the slide plus 4 feet. But slides taller than 10 feet don't need more than 14 feet. For swings, a safe landing zone is twice the height of the swing from the pivot point in the front and back.

Surfaces

Experts recommend installing a thick layer of shock-absorbent material under and around swings, slides, and other play equipment. Rubber mulch and foam mats offer the best cushioning and easy maintenance. Sand, pea gravel, and wood mulch are inexpensive mainstays, but be sure to get adequate depth. Sand needs to be broken up periodically to prevent compaction. Wood mulch needs to be replaced regularly. Don't forget: All surfaces require drainage.

sandboxes

S and play fascinates children. Add water and you're set for an afternoon . . . or days . . . or years. Situate your sandbox well to maximize enjoyment. You'll probably want a clear sight line from the house to supervise young children. Try to create a transition zone to prevent too much sand from ending up in the house.

SANDBOX INGREDIENTS Depth, size, and sand quality

Size and Depth

Kids will enjoy any size sandbox, but be sure the sand is at least 12 inches deep to allow room to dig. Sandboxes need a rim to contain the sand, so install an earthen berm or a wood, stone, brick, or concrete border. Leave the bottom of the box unenclosed, however, so water can drain out.

The Sand

Buy sand labeled for play. The best kind contains clean, rounded grains of the same small size. Ask for a grain size between 30 and 50 and with silt and clay content below 5 percent.

Cover

To keep cats and other animals out of the sandbox, use a cover when kids aren't there.

SUNSET CONTRIBUTING EDITOR
PETER O. WHITELEY ON
sand

>> Most commercial sand contains extremely fine shards of crystalline silica. Silica dust isn't good for lungs and has been linked to disease from long-term exposure. Look for sand that doesn't contain crystalline silica. Feldspar, for example, is a safe mineral. Also encourage kids to play in damp sand, which creates less dust.

All-purpose sand

Silica-free sand

Play sand

What an advantage, a field at home.

Space to run, kick, and throw may be all your child needs. A level field is versatile and open to possibility for any number of games, including golf, baseball, soccer, croquet, and volleyball. You can also set up a trampoline for the aspiring gymnast when you have large open spaces. In many cases you can purchase kits or gear that make staging a sport in the backyard effortless and economical. Or you can build equipment like a skateboard ramp from scratch. The degree of realism you bring to the endeavor—replicating the dimensions of a regulation soccer field or building a pitcher's mound—is up to you.

Coexist

Balance space for sports and games with space for adults and plants. There's room for everyone here, and diners can watch the action from ringside seats. Creating clear borders and protective walls or raised beds for plants helps reduce trampling. To make it convenient to go from one activity to another, and to preserve space for non-sport activities, consider equipment that is easy to move and store, such as a soccer goal. In addition to organized sports, don't forget classic games like tag or capture the flag that don't require large equipment.

Hardy Grass

Grass is beautiful and lush but also takes a lot of maintenance and water to keep it green. Before devoting a large amount of your backyard to grass, talk to your kids and make sure you believe it will be put to good use. Purchase grasses that can stand up to heavy foot traffic. Be sure to get what's appropriate to your climate and your yard's sun exposure. Also opt for pop-up sprinkler heads to avoid having anyone trip and fall.

Trampolines

Position trampolines far from other structures and on top of a soft, level landing surface. There should be 6 feet of clearance on all sides. While it's easier to install an aboveground trampoline on top of grass, an in-ground one built over a pit is safer. If you go for an elevated trampoline and have small children, opt for something that sits 1 to 2 feet off the ground. Ones for older kids and adults can be set higher. Cover the springs, pads, and hooks with thick foam padding to avoid injury and always supervise kids on trampolines. Trampoline enclosures are also available to prevent jumpers from falling off and younger kids and pets from climbing underneath.

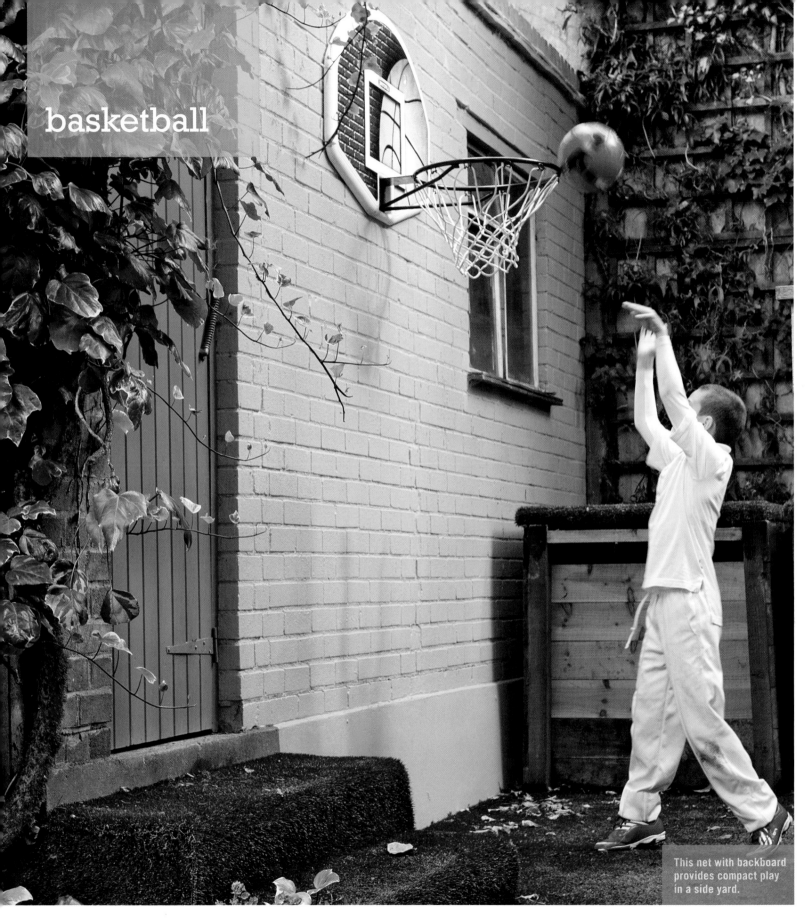

basketball

This net with backboard provides compact play in a side yard.

A basketball net can entertain children well through their teens. Mounted hoops don't take up a lot of space and can work well in small yards and driveways. Paint or draw a key on the ground below for authenticity. Teach kids to be respectful by only playing when neighbors are OK with the noise.

INSTALLING A BACKBOARD Steps to hoop dreams

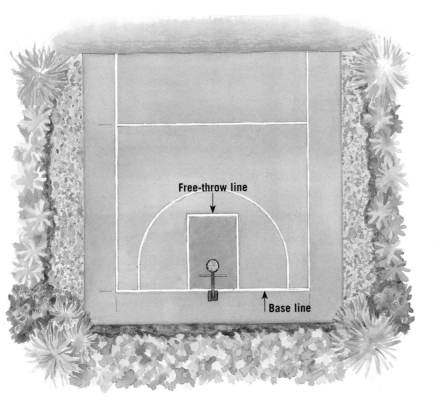

Court Space

Select a level, smooth, unobstructed playing surface, such as a driveway or patio. Regulation distance between the base line and the free-throw line is 19 feet. A regulation-size half court is 47 feet by 50 feet, but you'll have adequate practice space for free throws with a width of 12 feet. Purchase a rim, net, and backboard at a sporting goods or home improvement store. You may need to purchase mounting brackets separately. Regulation dimensions for a backboard are 72 by 42 inches, but you may want a smaller one. On a standard court, the middle of the net projects 63 inches forward from the base line.

Installation

You'll need a helper, as kit pieces are heavy. Regulation rim height is 10 feet. For wall-mounted backboards, as shown here, be sure that the net and rim extend beyond any over-hangs (such as roof soffits and rain gutters). Make sure the bracket is level and fasten it to wall studs with long lag screws. Attach the backboard to the brackets with carriage bolts. Install the hoop. For roof-mounted backboards, assemble brackets according to the manufacturer's instructions and fasten the brackets with lag screws through the roof and sheathing and into the rafters. Then seal the holes with roofing cement to prevent leaks.

swimming pools

1, 2, 3... jump in! Once safety standards are met, kids can focus on having a great time in the water.

Pools and water features are a delight—a natural draw for your kids and a bunch of friends. With pools and ponds, however, it's critical to put safety first. Supervise swimming children, maintaining a clear view of the entire pool. Install secure fencing so kids can't get to the water when you aren't there. Consider using rigid pool covers as well. For extra protection, there are water disturbance or wristband alarms that sound when a child is in the pool. Always keep lifesaving gear such as life preservers and a shepherd's pole nearby.

Fence It In

To prevent children from entering the pool without supervision, install a guardrail or fence that's at least 48 inches high and that lacks footholds that would allow for climbing. Pool gates should open out from the pool side and be self-latching and self-closing.

Cover

Covers are important safety features. Varieties include netting with holes too small for an infant to fall through, a strong polypropylene surface anchored to the sides of the pool, and a solid vinyl surface that you can roll out.

design lesson

>> Check with your city on the local building codes for fencing and safety regulations related to pools and ponds. Also check with your homeowners insurance policy holder regarding extra coverage that may be advisable.

Other Water Features

A pond or fountain can be just as dangerous for toddlers and infants as a pool. Safety covers can be designed to fit any pond shape.

A garden of his own makes strawberries even tastier.

Gardening with children is illuminating. Youngsters absorb the details of fresh buds and sweet scents. They often see things adults don't—because they're right at plant height. A great garden just takes a little bit of planning. To get started, sit down as a family to list and prioritize goals. Do you plan on growing produce or just flowers? Do your kids want their own vegetable patch or a butterfly garden? Will a pet need its own territory? Answering these questions will help you organize the garden into sections by function.

Get Whimsical

Add color and appeal with brightly painted structures. While this garden shed stores tools inside, its exterior is anything but workaday.

Make It Accessible

Low-growing plants can be reached easily by youngsters. Have your kids help by harvesting lettuces and herbs. Purchase scaled-down tools that fit in their small hands so they can dig in.

Express Wonder

Vining plants are just fun. And fast growers like these are clear evidence of the magic of it all. Help your children connect by linking plants to familiar stories such as "Jack and the Beanstalk."

Put Them to Work

Don't hesitate to give older children real garden tasks. They'll appreciate the satisfaction of accomplishment.

Close the Loop: Dine Well

Harvesting, of course, is the really fun part. Get kids involved with that—and with preparing and eating the fruits of their labor.

Involve your children in
your garden chores.

Enthrall your family with green space by nurturing a garden rich with color, texture, and a variety of forms. Choose plants that appeal most to you, as your enthusiasm will be apparent to the rest of your family and will likely rub off. Use the garden to teach your children about the whole connectedness of soil, air, water, animals, and people.

FAMILY FAVORITES Top picks for kids

Large, fast-growing, and colorful varieties are natural draws to children.

Bush Beans
Vining plant and a fast grower

Cosmos
Attracts hummingbirds

Fuchsias
Rich colors; hanging flowers are fairy-like

Hollyhocks
Spires can tower over kids

Lamb's Ear
Soft to the touch

Nasturtiums
Fast growing, edible

Pumpkins and Gourds
Good for crafts and holidays

Snapdragons
Attract hummingbirds; blooms look like little faces

Sunflowers
Tall, colorful, grow fast; let seeds form to attract birds

Tomatoes
Fun to harvest; choose cherry sizes

SUNSET GARDEN EDITOR
KATHLEEN NORRIS BRENZEL ON

plants to avoid

» Thorns or other prickly parts make these plants unfriendly: bougainvillea, cactus, roses.

» These plants are wholly or partially poisonous: brugmansia or angel's trumpet, delphiniums, foxglove, holly, hydrangea, mistletoe, oleander, wisteria.

think ahead

Your family and how you spend time together will change over the years.

In our happiest moments, we want to freeze time with our family. But of course there's no stopping that forward motion. Your family will grow up! Plan for the good times ahead by incorporating your changing needs and interests into today's designs for your backyard. You can't stop time, but you can definitely make room for future fun.

DESIGNED TO ADAPT   Same space, new uses

Grow and Flourish

Today's irresistible jungle tunnel becomes next season's veggie trellis. Repurposing items large and small allows your space to adapt with minimal effort. A backyard is a dynamic space; embrace how it changes over time.

Season to Season

Don't forget to consider how your backyard use changes through the seasons. Fall evenings come earlier than summer nights, but you will still want to enjoy them outside with your family. Consider how the light changes through the year and build into your plans outdoor lighting, weather protection, and activities for warm days and cold.

Let Them Sing Their Own Tune

You can't predict where your children's interests will take them, but you can give them room to explore. Provide the opportunity for discovery with a safe play space that has tools and toys that foster creativity. Unstructured playtime can spark the imagination.

Playhouse to Workhouse

A playhouse that sometimes hosts tea parties becomes a homework center. There are many possibilities for adapting a structure to new functions: playhouse to…toolshed, greenhouse, mini theater, workroom, art studio, wine cellar, guest room, yoga studio. The list goes on.

19

The following organizations, manufacturers, and retailers are mentioned or have products shown in this book. They can help to plan, design, and stock your new backyard play area.

Associations and Organizations

American Society of Landscape Architects
www.asla.org

American Youth Soccer Organization
www.soccer.org

Association of Professional Landscape Designers
www.apld.com

Backyard Chickens
www.backyardchickens.com

Building Materials Reuse Association
www.bmra.org

Consumer Product Safety Commission
www.cpsc.gov

Forest Stewardship Council
www.fsc.org

Green Roofs
www.greenroofs.com

Youth Basketball of America
www.yboa.org

Structures

HomePlace Structures
www.homeplacestructures.com

Pacific Play Tents
www.pacificplaytents.com

Swing-n-Slide
www.swing-n-slide.com

TreeHouse Workshop
www.treehouseworkshop.com

Materials

All-Safe Pool Safety Products
www.allsafepool.com

Backyard Sports Center
www.backyardsportscenter.com

Green Depot
www.greendepot.com

The Home Depot
www.homedepot.com

IKEA
www.ikea.com

Katch a Kid Pool Covers
www.katchakid.com

Lowe's
www.lowes.com

Renee's Garden
www.reneesgarden.com

Safe Sand Company
www.safesand.com

Seeds of Change
www.seedsofchange.com

Sunbrella
www.sunbrella.com

Thompson's Waterseal
www.thompsonswaterseal.com

Photography

Alan Abraham/Corbis: 46; Melanie Acevedo/Getty Images: 114 (design: Nonchalant Mom Fashion Design); ACP + Syndication: 73, 102, 104 all, 105, 124, 125, 126, 127 all; Altrendo Images/Getty Images: 51 top; Monica Bach/Pure Public/Living Inside: 13 both; Bill Bachmann/Photo Network: 75 right; Leander Baerenz/Getty Images: 63 bottom; John Bendtsen/Pure Public/Living Inside: 47 top; Robert J. Bennett: 75 left; Marion Brenner: 37 top, 49 top, 167 top #3, 167 top #5; David Brittain/Ideal Home/IPC Media: 142 left; Jason Busch/ACP/trunkarchive.com: 169 bottom right; Reggie Casagrande/Getty Images: 39 bottom; Roger Charity/Getty Images: 41 bottom; Ian van Coller/Getty Images: 165 bottom center; Beatriz da Costa: 52; courtesy of Cover Pools: 163 top right; Jack Coyier: 110 (design: Richard Krumwiede, Architerra Design Group), 120 (design: Richard Krumwiede, Architerra Design Group); Cultura/Floresco Productions/Getty Images: 63 top; Alan & Linda Detrick: 155 right; Dan Duchars/Living Etc./IPC + Syndication: 44; Paul Dudley/Amateur Gardening/IPC + Syndication: 28; Liz Eddison/The Garden Collection: 157 bottom left; Sam Eddison/The Garden Collection: 67 bottom; Scott Fitzgerrell: 76 bottom right center; Thomas Fricke/Getty Images: 23 bottom left; Frank Gaglione: 77 bottom left center, 113 right; William Geddes: 36; Tria Giovan: 24 top, 43, 148 both; Tria Giovan/Photoshot/Red Cover: 119 left; Lena Granefelt/Getty Images: front cover; John Granen: 140; Art Gray: 118; A. Green/Corbis: 74; Steven A. Gunther: 174; Jerry Harpur/Harpur Garden Images: 18, (design: Christopher Masson), 23 top (design: Bunny Guinness), 153 bottom left, 157 top left (design: Ryl Nowell), 163 bottom, 165 top right; Marcus Harpur/Harpur Garden Images: 14 (design: Nick Williams-Ellis), 58, (design: Lesley Faux), 60 top (design: Dr. Mary Giblin), 61 (design: Lesley Faux), 139 bottom left, 159 top right (design: Justin Greer), 159 bottom (design: Justin Greer), 164, 169 top left (design: Lucy Redman), 169 top right (design: Yulia Badian); Modeste Herwig/The Garden Collection: 163 top left; Jackie Hobbs/The Garden Collection: 20 (design: Bunny Guinness); Maree Homer/ACP/trunkarchive.com: 21 bottom; IPC + Syndication: 93 both; Bjarni B. Jacobsen/Living Inside: 42; Johner/Getty Images: 147 bottom left; Pernille Kaalund/Pure Public/Living Inside: 49 both; Simon Kenny/Content-agency/Living Inside: 31, 57 top, 153; Jutta Klee/Getty Images: 60 bottom; James Knowler/ACP/trunkarchive.com: 11, 45 top; Chuck Kuhn: 78 (designed and built by Bob Stanton), 80 both, 81 all, 83 all, 94 (design: TreeHouse Workshop), 96 both, 97 all, 99 all, 100 both (design: TreeHouse Workshop); Eva Kylland/Living Inside: 48; Andrew Lawson/MMGI: 29 bottom left; Tom Leighton/Country Homes & Interiors/IPC + Syndication: 147 top left, 147 bottom right; Chris Leschinsky: 25, 62, 139 bottom right, 158; Marianne Majerus/MMGI: 15 (design: Ivan Hicks), 17 both, 19 top left, 19 top right, 23 bottom right, 26, 34, 35 both, 37 bottom, 38, 41 top, 45 bottom, 49 bottom, 50, 138 (design: Stuart Craine), 145 top right (design: Elton Hall), 150 (design: Lynne Marcus), 153 top left, (design: Julie Toll), 159 top left (design: Ian Kitson), 160 (design: Jane Brockbank), 165 bottom left; Jennifer Martiné: 66, 68; Paul Massey/Living Etc./IPC + Syndication: 19 bottom; Paul Massey/Living Etc./IPC Media: 142 right; Simon McBride/Red Cover/Photoshot: 12; Ericka McConnell: 7 top, 32, 40, 59, 65 top, 145 top left, 172; Paul McGee/Getty Images: 33 bottom; Laura Moss: 9 bottom; Emily Nathan: 166; Mike Newling: 1, 2, 3 left, 5, 7 bottom, 10 bottom right, 47 bottom, 71, 72, 84 (design: Keith Willig Landscape Architecture and Construction), 86 (design: Keith Willig Landscape Architecture and Construction), 87 both (design: Keith Willig Landscape Architecture and Construction), 88 (design: Roch Soensken Design), 90 both (design: Roch Soensken Design), 91 bottom left (design: Roch Soensken Design), 128 (design: Peter O. Whiteley and Jack Halloway), 130 both, 131 all, 132 (design: Alex Hodgkinson, McCutcheon Construction), 135, 143 right, 144, 146, 147 top right, back cover left, 170; Jerry Pavia/Red Cover/Photoshot: 8, 165 top left, 165 top center; courtesy of Peltor Kid: 77 bottom right center; Alejandro Peral/Living Inside: 53 (design: Remy Arq); Costas Picadas/Gap Interiors: 24 bottom; Norm Plate: 123 both (design: David C. Becker); Norman A. Plate: 167 top #1, 167 bottom #4, 167 bottom #5; Spike Powell/Country Homes and Interiors/IPC + Syndication: 56; Lisa Romerein: 51 bottom; Eric Roth: 55 bottom; Prue Ruscoe/ACP/trunkarchive.com: 64; Prue Ruscoe/Taverne Agency: 27, 55 top, 168; Mark Scott/Ideal Home/IPC + Syndication: 67 top; Bennet Smith/MMGI: 16, 29 top, 29 bottom right, 139 top left, back cover bottom right; Martin Solyst/Living Inside: 33 top, 143 left; Carl De Souza/Getty Images: 65 bottom; SPC Photo Collection: 167 bottom #3; Derek St. Romaine/The Garden Collection: 39 top; Hugh Stewart/ACP/trunkarchive.com: 30, 69, 169 bottom left, back cover top right; Thomas J. Story: 3 right, 76 top left, 76 top left center, 76 top right center, 76 top right, 76 bottom left, 76 bottom left center, 76 bottom right, 77 top row all, 77 bottom left, 92 (design: Trisha Olson, Out-N-In Tents), 116, (design: Peter O. Whiteley), 119 right (design: Levy Art & Architecture), 137, 141 bottom, 156, 157 top right (design: EDI Architecture), 157 bottom right, 162, 167 top #2, 167 top #4, 167 bottom #1, 167 bottom #2; Tim Street-Porter: 6, 9 top; Sue Stubbs/ACP/trunkarchive.com: 152; Dave Toht: 113 left; Nicola Stocken Tomkins/The Garden Collection: 10 top, 10 bottom left; TreeHouse Workshop: 22 (design: TreeHouse Workshop); Chris Tubbs/Red Cover/Photoshot: 21 top; Michael Wee/ACP/trunkarchive.com: 154; Michael Wee/Red Cover/Photoshot: 54; Lee Anne White: 155 left; Michele Lee Willson: 106 (design: Swing-N-Slide Playsets), 108 all, 109 all, 139 top right (design: Kelly Bowman Greenwood); Mel Yates/Living Etc./IPC + Syndication: 57 bottom

Illustration

Tracy La Rue Hohn: 161 both; Melanie Powell/Studio in the Woods: 141 all, 145 both; Damien Scogin: 80, 82, 87 all, 91, 96 both, 98, 105 all, 112 both, 117 all, 122, 126 all, 130 both, 134

index